A LONGMAN
LATIN READER

THE AULULARIA OF PLAUTUS

The Pot of Gold

D1611295

Prepared by Gilbert Lawall and Betty Nye Quinn

LONGMAN

The Aulularia of Plautus: The Pot of Gold

Longman ,10 Bank Street, White Plains, N.Y. 10606

Associated companies:
Longman Group Ltd., London
Longman Cheshire Pty., Melbourne
Longman Paul Pty., Auckland
Copp Clark Pitman, Toronto
Pitman Publishing Inc., New York

Authors: **Professor Gilbert Lawall**, University of Massachusetts,
Amherst, Massachusetts
Professor Betty Nye Quinn, Mount Holyoke College,
South Hadley, Massachusetts
Series Editor: **Professor Gilbert Lawall**
Consultants: **Jane Harriman Hall**, Mary Washington College,
Fredericksburg, Virginia
Richard A. LaFleur, University of Georgia,
Athens, Georgia
Robert E. Morse, Saint Andrew's School,
Boca Raton, Florida

Executive editor: Lyn McLean
Production editor: Elsa van Bergen
Text and cover designer: Gayle Jaeger
Production supervisor: Judith Stern

ISBN 0-582-36753-0

Compositor: r/tsi typographic company, inc.

26 17

CONTENTS

ACKNOWLEDGMENTS

Some of the comprehension questions in the student's book and some of the discussion questions in the notes in the teacher's handbook are based on questions formulated by the following students in Latin 691A, History of Latin Literature, taught by Professor Gilbert Lawall at the University of Massachusetts at Amherst in fall, 1985: Donald Benander, Sharon Montague deFriesse, Mary Gardner, Anita Jog, Claire Mazzola, Kathleen McCarthy, Barbara Romaine, and Andrew Schacht. Some of the material in the Introduction to the student's book has been borrowed from *Plautus' Menaechmi*: Edited with Introduction and Running Vocabularies by Gilbert Lawall and Betty Nye Quinn (Bolchazy-Carducci Publishers, Chicago, 1982).

INTRODUCTION

Titus Maccius Plautus was born about 254 B.C. and died about 184 B.C. The most successful comic poet of his time, he wrote in the medium of the contemporary Roman stage, which means that he adapted in Latin for his Roman audience the plays of the post-classical Greek theater.

Easily supplanting the formless and nonliterary Italic dramatic skits, the highly developed Greek drama—tragedy as well as comedy—captured the Roman stage in the third century B.C. Southern Italy and Sicily had been settled by Greek colonists in the great waves of overseas colonization that had begun in the eighth century. Commercial and cultural contacts of Rome with Magna Graecia, as southern Italy was called by the Romans, had developed during Rome's defensive war in the early third century on behalf of some of the southern cities against the Greek invader Pyrrhus of Epirus, a kinsman of Alexander the Great. During the first of Rome's prolonged and perilous wars with Carthage (264–241 B.C.), fought in the decade before Plautus' birth and during his childhood, Roman legions campaigned through southern Italy and Sicily, and the ordinary soldier gleaned his first taste of Greek civilization, sophistication, and entertainment. In the long and hazardous twenty years of fighting in the Second Punic War (218–201 B.C.) when Hannibal came dangerously close to conquering Rome, the Roman legions again marched and fought steadily throughout southern Italy, where early in the war the majority of cities had cast their lot with Hannibal, the destroyer of three Roman armies in three years. During the last years of Plautus' activity, a dozen legions were dispatched across the Adriatic for campaigns against the kings of Macedon and Syria.

Exultation over the national victory in the First Punic War (241 B.C.) created the climate for the birth of literature in Rome. Rome's continued conquests meant unprecedented economic advance, a progress in things material matched by progress in things of the mind. The importation of Greek culture, amenities, and depravities (as some Greek customs were viewed from the Roman point of view) is apt to conceal the fact that the real stimulus to produce a Roman literature came from national achievement and national needs. Roman demands for education and amusement required that Greek epic and drama should be adapted to contemporary tastes. Talented poets who could imitate Greek models in Latin were henceforth ensured a sympathetic hearing.

The two wars with Carthage strained Rome's manpower to the very limit so that practically every adult male in Rome, and indeed in Italy, had seen service in Greek-speaking regions of Italy and Sicily. The man-in-the-Roman-street had experienced and acquired a taste for Greek culture, had learned a few Greek words, and was ready for entertainment a cut above that of the ordinary slapstick buffoonery of the traditional home fare. The first play modeled on a Greek prototype was written by Livius Andronicus, a Greek brought to Rome from Tarentum in southern Italy, and was produced at Rome in 240 B.C. at games celebrating the triumphant close of the First Punic

War. Its reception was gratifying, and the audience clearly demanded more of the same. Plays came to be performed regularly as part of the free popular entertainment offered at the celebration of religious games, and they ran in competition with horse races, acrobats, dancers, and various side-shows. The games were produced by elected officials, the aediles, who expected the success of the games to further their political careers.

GREEK NEW COMEDY IN ROME

These new dramas with well-defined and often intricate plots were called **fābulae palliātae** ("stories in Greek dress") to distinguish them from the formless repartee of Italic comedy. They comprised Latin translations, adaptations, and reworkings of Greek originals, for here as in other literary and philosophic areas the Romans assimilated, revitalized, and transmitted Greek thought and achievement for the immediate Roman society and for the subsequent Western world. In terms of the history and evolution of Greek comedy as a genre, the comedy to which Rome fell heir is known to literary historians as New Comedy, a product of the urbane, cosmopolitan upper-middle-class Athenian society of the late fourth and early third centuries B.C. It represented a uniform social pattern and was compassionate in its treatment and characterized by a gentle sentimentality. The greatest writer of this Athenian New Comedy was Menander (ca. 342–298 B.C.). Long perished were the freedom of speech and the patriotic spirit which had been the very essence of the Athenian Old Comedy of the fifth century, exemplified by Aristophanes (ca. 450–385 B.C.) and characterized by partisan political crusades, indirect or even direct abuse of living notables, didactic preaching, satirical calls for reform, ribald obscenities, mythological characters, and fanciful settings. The Middle Comedy of the first three-quarters of the fourth century provided a muted transition to New Comedy, in which the man-next-door walked the stage. Subject matter and dramatic conflict, like the characters, are now commonplace and rely on coincidence, chance, and intrigue rather than upon fantasy, divine intervention, or forces larger than life. Plots revolve around domestic problems and the love affairs of young men and their fathers, often involving courtesans and cases of mistaken identity.

Since the first permanent stone theater in Rome was not built until 55 B.C., it is not clear where earlier plays were presented: perhaps in temporary wooden structures on open ground, at the crossroads of city streets, or on the podium of a temple. The stage setting was usually a city street, onto which opened the doors of three houses; in many plays, as in our play, the *Aulularia* (*The Pot of Gold*), there was an altar on the stage. The exit on the right of the audience led to the forum, while that on the left led to the harbor or country. There were neither acts nor intermissions, so action was continuous; actual time and dramatic time were equal or nearly so. Like their Greek prototypes, the Roman plays were written in verse (never in prose). Some sections were written in meters to be delivered in ordinary conversational tones; other sections were in meters to be recited in more animated and emotional tones; then, unique to Roman comedy, there were lyric passages to be sung to the accompaniment of wind instruments. Passages for these three modes of delivery are designated DIALOGUE, RECITATIVE, and SONG, respectively, and the production of a Roman play would have resembled a modern light opera or musical comedy. The characters were the members of one or more families

2

and their confidantes, including slaves, friends, and parasites, as well as assorted professionals, such as courtesans, procurers, lawyers, doctors, and soldiers. The situation at the outset was often explained in a prologue. In the *Aulularia* the prologue is spoken by the household god, the **Lar familiāris** (a Roman god, although the scene of this play is set in Athens), who claims to be manipulating the plot. The troupe of actors was limited in numbers, and actors, probably slaves, regularly played more than one role. Women's parts were taken by men: ladies wore white or yellow and courtesans saffron. Old men wore white wigs and slaves red ones. Whether the actors wore masks is an open question.

In transplanting Greek New Comedy to a Roman audience, playwrights preserved much of the original. The scene remains Greek, usually Athenian. The characters have Greek names, often descriptive of their nature but sometimes at odds with it. In the *Aulularia*, the notorious miser is named **Eucliō** "Of Good Fame"; the mother, a staid matron with old Roman values, is named **Eunomia** "Good Order"; and her brother, a wealthy and generous bachelor, is **Megadōrus** "Great Giver." The clothes are Greek as well; freemen wear the Greek **pallium** or cloak over a tunic (hence the Roman term for these plays, **fābulae palliātae**), slaves wear sleeveless tunics, and women wear the *chitôn* or long gown. Un-Roman, indeed, must have appeared the scant respect shown for old age and the familiarity and trickery of slaves, who are usually depicted as much smarter than their masters. The Romans, somewhat puritanical, stiff-necked, sober, and naive, felt their curiosity stirred by representations of adultery, sexual aberrations, and intrigues against that august figure, the **pater familiās**. However, as long as faults and foibles, knavery and intrigue were portrayed as Greek and not Roman, they could amuse and not offend.

Yet throughout runs a purely Roman touch. There is Roman severity in the threatened punishments of whip and cross and a Roman coarseness in the emphasis laid on the pleasures of eating, drinking, and sex. There is an abundance of Latin puns, Roman customs, Roman attitudes, and Roman references—topographical, historical, religious, civic, and legal. The world of Roman comedy is one that never actually existed—an amalgam of Greek and Roman locales, characters, and ideas. This is how all the early Roman playwrights (such as Livius Andronicus and Gnaeus Naevius) adapted their Greek models, but Plautus brought his own sure touch, his intimacy with earthy Italian dramatic fare, and probably his personal experiences as an actor upon the boards.

PLAUTUS

Biographical details about Plautus are scant and may be subject to suspicion. Even his tripartite Roman name (**Titus Maccius Plautus**) has been questioned: some scholars have suggested that Plautus or Plotus was his Umbrian nickname meaning "Flatfoot" or "Dog-eared" and that Maccus, later changed to Maccius, was the regular name of the clown, a role Plautus is said to have played in Italic farces when he came to Rome.

Plautus was born in the small town of Sarsinna in Umbria, a district far north of Rome along the Adriatic Sea. He came to Rome and turned to theatrical work, perhaps continuing a profession he had followed in his native town, and presumably joined a touring company of traveling actors presenting impromptu entertainment of the Italic folk variety.

This popular comedy of a rough and rollicking sort had been amusing Italians and Romans long before the literate Greek importations made their appearance.

How this Umbrian learned Latin so well and mastered Greek sufficiently to become familiar with his Greek models is unknown. Possibly he attended a school in the Greek colony of Ancona on the coast near Sarsinna. He did, however, leave us a legacy of twenty-one plays, perhaps only a small portion of his total output.

PLAUTUS' INFLUENCE

Annual presentations of Plautine plays by various schools, colleges, and universities in both Latin and English testify to the enduring vitality of Roman comedy and to the versatile appeal of Plautus across the centuries. Shakespeare based his *Comedy of Errors* (ca. 1591) on Plautus' *Menaechmi* and *Amphitryon*, changing the locale, adding a second set of twins, furnishing more romantic interest, and providing a happier ending with the survival and reunion of the twins' parents. Ben Jonson's *The Alchemist* (1610) recalls various details of Plautus' *Mostellaria*. In France, Molière drew on the *Aulularia* for his *L'Avare* (*The Miser*, 1668), creating in the title role of Harpagon a memorable picture of an unreformed miser. Selections from Molière's play are given in English translation in the Passages for Comparison at the end of this book. Broadway too has profited from Plautus with *Amphitryon 38*, a play by Giraudoux based on Plautus' *Amphitryon*; *The Boys from Syracuse* (1938), a musical from Plautus' *Menaechmi* via Shakespeare and a perennial favorite of summer and dinner theaters; and *A Funny Thing Happened on the Way to the Forum*, a pastiche of Plautine plots which enjoyed success as a movie as well.

THE *AULULARIA*

Whereas the original Greek play probably centered upon the love story of Lyconides and Phaedria and the ultimate happy ending, Plautus chose to emphasize the comic character of her miserly father Euclio, for whose antics the romance is only a backdrop. Although his household god, the **Lar familiāris**, states in the prologue that all is being arranged to ensure a dowry and proper marriage for Phaedria, the action of the play revolves around the miserliness of Euclio. This perversity of his character, exaggerated nearly beyond credible proportion, is illustrated in his relations with his slave Staphyla, his mistrust of his wealthy neighbor and would-be son-in-law, Megadorus, his reaction to the cooks hired for the wedding, his attempts to hide his treasure, and his frenzied grief when it is stolen. Unfortunately, the end of the play has been lost so we do not know exactly how Plautus resolved the situation. It is, however, clear from the two summaries, which appear in the manuscripts (and are the work of grammarians of the Empire who had the full text of the play), that the lovers will be united in marriage and that the miserly Euclio after a change of heart gives his pot of gold as his daughter's dowry, fulfilling the words of the Lar in the prologue. For a similar interweaving of a romantic plot and a character study, one may compare Menander's only extant play, the *Dyskolos* (*The Grouch*), selections from which are given in English translation in the Passages for Comparison at the end of this book.

LANGUAGE

The Latin that Plautus wrote shows many features of the early or archaic stage in the development of the language, such as the ending **-os** in the nominative singular of certain 2nd declension nouns (**auos** = **avus**), **-o-** instead of **-e-** in the stems of some words (**vortant** = **vertant**), the ending **-āī** in the genitive singular of 1st declension nouns (**fīliāī** = **fīliae**), passive infinitives ending in **-ier** (**adferrier** = **adferrī**), unassimilated prefixes as in the previous example, subjunctive forms such as **siet** = **sit**, **duit** = **det**, and **faxint** = **fēcerint**, and words beginning with **q-** instead of **c-** (**qūr** = **cūr**, **quius** = **cuius**, and **quom** = **cum** as a conjunction). In lowercase letters no distinction was made between *u* and *v*; both were written as **u**, as in **auos** = **avus**; as capitals, both appeared as **V**.

In the present edition of the play, these features of early Latin have been eliminated, and the spellings used are those that you will be familiar with from your previous study of the language. This has been done to allow you to read the play with a minimum of difficulty and to focus your attention on the play itself, its plot and characters, without being distracted by unusual spellings of otherwise familiar Latin words and forms.

You should be alerted, however, to a few archaic forms of the language that have been preserved in this edition and to some features of formal or poetic Latin that will be encountered both in this play and in other literary works of all periods:

1. The suffix **-ce** or **-c** is added to some demonstrative pronouns and adjectives for extra emphasis. It is already familiar from **hic, haec, hoc**. In Plautus the suffix is still added to forms from which it disappeared in later Latin; thus, we find **hōsce** for **hōs** and **hāsce** for **hās**. When this suffix is added to **ille, illa, illud**, we get **illic, illaec, illuc**. When added to **iste, ista, istud**, we get **istic, istaec, istuc**. Just remember that the **-ce** or **-c** is added for emphasis; forms that might be confusing are identified in the facing vocabularies.
2. The word **quī** will sometimes be found as an old ablative form used as an adverb ("how?" "how so?") or used to introduce a purpose clause ("in order that by this means"). These usages will be indicated in the notes.
3. The word **cedo** will be found as an old imperative form meaning "give!"
4. The words **sī vīs** "if you wish," "please," are contracted to **sīs**, which can be confused with the present subjunctive of **sum**. Again, the notes will help.
5. Sometimes the pluperfect indicative is used where we would expect a simple perfect tense, and the future perfect is used where we would expect a simple future tense.
6. The word **ecce** "look!" "behold!" is combined with forms of the pronoun **is, ea, id** to give forms like **eccum** (= **ecce eum**) "here he is!" or **eccās** (= **ecce eās**) "here they are!"
7. Forms of the future imperative will be met (e.g., **astātō** "stand there!") often as simple imperatives with no future sense.
8. The abbreviated form **mī** is often used for **mihi**. The alternative 2nd person singular passive ending **-re** is often used instead of **-ris** (e.g., **exstinguēre** = **exstinguēris**). And, with 3rd declension nouns and adjectives the alternative accusative plural ending **-īs** is often used (e.g., **omnīs** = **omnēs**). (Note that this alternative ending is never used for the

nominative plural and that it is therefore easily possible to distinguish the nominative from the accusative plural of these 3rd declension nouns and adjectives.)

None of these forms should cause any trouble, and ample help is always at hand in the notes facing the Latin text.

READING AND PERFORMING THE PLAY

This is a play to be read aloud and acted out. Each page of Latin text makes a convenient segment that can be read and acted in class. Only when the scenes are acted out will you fully appreciate the humor, force, and irony of the dramatic encounters between the characters. The audience, too, is part of the comedy, and those reading and acting the parts should always play to the audience as well as to the other characters on the make-believe classroom stage. Bring the play to life in your classroom, just as the ancients brought it to life in the streets of Rome.

Two short adaptations of the play are available for those wishing to stage a more formal production. One, *The Pot of Gold*, is a version that can be performed in 15 minutes, in simplified Latin. The other, *Plautus' Aulularia: The Pot of Gold: An Adaptation for Production by High School Latin Students*, is a longer version (about 50 minutes), with an English prologue and English lead-ins and bridge passages interspersed with an adapted version of the Latin text. Both adaptations have endings (the ending of Plautus' original play, you will remember, has been lost); either adaptation can be effectively staged and presented for the enjoyment of first- and second-year as well as of more advanced Latin students.

Staphyla and Euclio

6

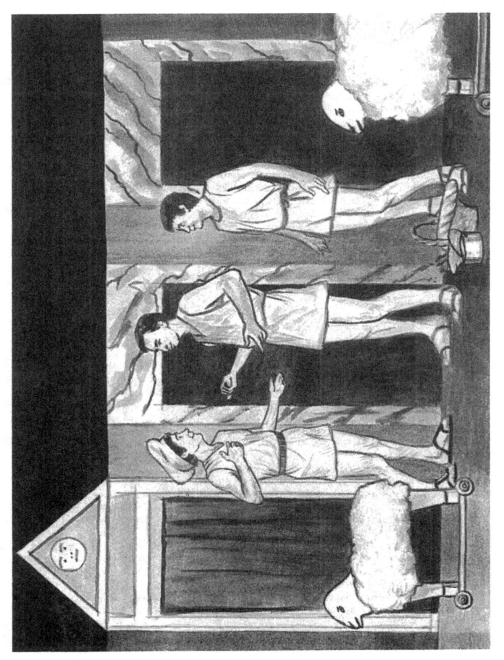

Strobilus (center) with the two cooks, the sheep, and provisions for dinner

DRAMATIS PERSONAE

Lar familiāris, the god of Euclio's household
Eucliō, an old man
Staphyla, Euclio's old slave woman
Eunomia, sister of Megadorus and mother of Lyconides
Megadōrus, Eunomia's brother, an elderly bachelor
Strobīlus, slave of Megadorus   **Eleusium**, flute girl
Anthrax, cook   **Lyconidis servus**, slave of Lyconides
Congriō, cook   **Lyconidēs**, a young man, son of Eunomia
Phrygia, flute girl   **Phaedria**, Euclio's daughter

---

1 *** quis**: = **aliquis** (after **nē**, introducing a negative purpose clause). **quī**: = **quis** (here introducing an indirect question).
   ***ēloquor, ēloquī** (3), **ēlocūtus sum**, to speak out, tell.
2 *** Lar, Laris** (*m*), the tutelary god of hearth and home.
3 *** exeō, exīre** (*irreg.*), **exīvī** or **exiī, exitum**, to come or go out.
   ***aspiciō, aspicere** (3), **aspexī, aspectum**, to catch sight of, observe.
4 **iam multōs annōs est cum possideō. . . .**: "it's many years now that I (have) inhabit(ed). . . ."
   possideō, possidēre (2), **possēdī, possessum**, to hold, occupy, inhabit.
   ***colō, colere** (3), **coluī, cultum**, to live in, cultivate, tend.
5 *** avus, -ī** (*m*), grandfather.
   ***habitō** (1), to live, dwell.
6 *** obsecrō** (1), to pray, implore, beg.
   ***concrēdō, concrēdere** (3), **concrēdidī, concrēditum**, to entrust something to someone (dative) for safekeeping.
7 *** aurum, -ī** (*n*), gold.
   ***thēsaurus, -ī** (*m*) (*Greek loan word*), hoard, treasure, store.
   ***omnīs**: = **omnēs** (acc. pl.).
   ***focus, -ī** (*m*), the hearth or fireplace in the **ātrium**, the center of the worship of the **Lar familiāris**.
8 *** dēfodiō, dēfodere** (3), **dēfōdī, defossum**, to bury (by digging down).
   veneror, venerārī (1), **venerātus sum**, to worship, beg. **venerāns**: what kind of clause does this participle introduce? **id**: "the secret."
9 **quoniam**: = **postquam**.
   morior, morī (3), **mortuus sum**, to die. ***avidus, -a, -um**, greedy, avaricious.
   ingenium, -ī (*n*), inborn character. **avidō ingeniō**: ablative of description.
10 *** indicō** (1), to reveal, declare.
11 **inops, inopis**, lacking wealth (**opēs, opum**, *f pl*), poor, destitute.
   optō (1), to wish, desire. ***potius . . . quam** (12), rather than.
12 **commōnstrō** (1), to point out, show where something is. **commōnstrāret**: subjunctive in a substantive clause of purpose (without **ut**) parallel to the infinitive **relinquere** (11), both dependent on **optāvit potius**, "he preferred."
14 **quō**: here, "so that thereby," introducing a purpose clause.
15 *** obeō, obīre** (*irreg.*), **obīvī** or **obiī, obitum**, to meet with, come up against. **mortem** or **diem obīre**, to meet one's death, die. ***mī**: = **mihi**.
16 *** observō** (1), to observe, note.
   ecquī (*adverbial abl.*), whether in any way (introducing an indirect question). Note that **quī** here and often elsewhere in Plautus is an old ablative form.
17 **habuisset**: subjunctive by attraction.
18 *** vērō**, truly. ***minus**, less.
   impendium, -ī (*n*), expense, cost. **impendiō**: here ablative as adverb, "greatly," "very much." **minus impendio**: "much less."
19 **cūrāre . . . impertīre**: historical infinitives, equivalent to past tenses of the indicative, with subject **ille** (18).
   impertiō (4), to present someone (accusative) with a share of something (ablative).
21 **hunc**: with **fīlium** at the end of the line.
22 **pariter**, equally, in the same manner.
   ***mōrātus, -a, -um**, endowed with character or manners (**mōrēs**) of a specified kind.

THE AULULARIA OF PLAUTUS

The scene is a city street in Athens showing the closed doors of three buildings. In the center is the house of Euclio, on the audience's right the house of Megadorus, and on the left the temple of Fides. An altar to Apollo stands in the center toward the front of the stage. From the house of Euclio appears the Lar familiāris, *a young, slender figure clad in high boots, short tunic, and belted undergarment. Garlands adorn his head. Lithe and graceful, he moves nimbly about as he speaks.*

1	**LAR** Nē quis mirētur quī sim, paucīs ēloquar.	DIALOGUE
2	Ego Lar sum familiāris ex hāc familiā (*pointing to Euclio's house*)	
3	unde exeuntem mē aspexistis. Hanc domum	
4	iam multōs annōs est cum possideō et colō	
5	patrī avōque iam huius quī nunc hīc habitat.	
6	Sed mihi avus huius obsecrāns concrēdidit	
7	aurī thēsaurum clam omnīs: in mediō focō	
8	dēfōdit, venerāns mē ut id servārem sibi.	
9	Is quoniam moritur, (ita avidō ingeniō fuit)	
10	numquam indicāre id filiō voluit suō,	
11	inopemque optāvit potius eum relinquere	
12	quam eum thēsaurum commōnstrāret filiō;	
13	agrī relīquit eī nōn magnum modum,	
14	quō cum labōre magnō et miserē vīveret.	
15	Ubi is obiit mortem quī mī id aurum crēdidit,	
16	coepī observāre, ecquī maiōrem filius	
17	mihi honōrem habēret quam eius habuisset pater.	
18	Atque ille vērō minus minusque impendiō	
19	cūrāre minusque mē impertīre honōribus.	
20	Item ā mē contrā factum est, nam item obiit diem.	
21	Is ex sē hunc relīquit quī hīc nunc habitat filium	
22	pariter mōrātum ut pater avusque huius fuit.	

1. Why does the Lar tell us who he is? (1)
2. Of what family is he the Lar? (2–3)
3. How long has he been the Lar of that house? (4–5)
4. What did Euclio's grandfather entrust to the Lar? (6–7)
5. Where did the grandfather hide it? (7) With what attitude toward the Lar? (6–8)
6. What kind of a man was the grandfather? (9)
7. What did this character trait of his cause him to do? (10–12)
8. What did he leave to his son? (13–14)
9. What did the Lar do after the death of the grandfather? (16–17)
10. How did the son treat the Lar? (18–19)
11. Whom does the Lar mean by *hunc filium*? (21)
12. What does the Lar mean by the phrase *pariter mōrātum*? (22)

23 **fīlia**: Phaedria, who has one and a half lines at 691–692.
24 **tūs, tūris** (*n*), incense.
  aliquī (*adverbial abl.*), in some other way, with something else.
  supplicō (1), to pray to, worship, supplicate. The Lar was honored at meals with part of the food. Special sacrifices were offered at the Kalends, Nones, and Ides, as well as at various family celebrations.
25 *corōna, -ae** (*f*), wreath. *grātiā** (+ *gen.*), out of consideration for, for the purpose of.
26 **reperīret**: subjunctive in a substantive clause of result.
27 **quō**: here = **ut** (in a purpose clause containing a comparative adverb).
  *nūbō, nūbere** (3), **nūpsī, nūptum**, (of a woman) to get married to. *nūptum dare**, to give (someone) in marriage.
28 *comprimō, comprimere** (3), **compressī, compressum**, to press tightly, make love with, rape.
29 **sit**: why subjunctive? **compresserit**: subjunctive by attraction.
30 *nescio** (4), not to know. **neque . . . autem**: "nor on the other hand."
31 **Eam . . . uxōrem** (32): "her as his wife." *senex, senis** (*m*), old man (i.e., Megadorus).
  *proximum, -ī** (*n*), the immediate neighborhood or vicinity. **dē** or **ex proximō**, from close at hand, neighboring, next door.
32 **eā . . . grātiā**: "for this purpose," "for her sake."
33 **quō**: = **ut** (as in line 27).
  dūcat: supply **in mātrimōnium**. *mātrimōnium, -ī** (*n*), marriage. **compresserat**: pluperfect for perfect.
34 **hic**: **senex** (end of the line).
35 *avunculus, -ī** (*m*), mother's brother, maternal uncle.
36 **stuprō** (1), to defile, dishonor. *Cerēs, Cereris** (*f*), the goddess of agriculture.
  *vigilia, -ae** (*f*), wakefulness, watching, (military) guard, (here) nightly vigils at the religious festival of Ceres.
37 *intus** (*adv.*), inside.
38 *anus, -ūs** (*f*), old woman. *forās**, out of doors (always implying motion).
  *extrūdō, extrūdere** (3), **extrūsī, extrūsum**, to force to go out, eject, expel.
  nē sit: what kind of a clause? **cōnscius, -a, -um**, sharing (secret) knowledge, in the know.
39 *īnspiciō, īnspicere** (3), **īnspexī, īnspectum**, to examine, inspect.
  *surripiō, surripere** (3), **surripuī, surreptum**, to snatch away secretly, steal.
40 *age**, come now! come on! *hercle**, by Hercules!
41 **circumspectātrix, circumspectātricis** (*f*), a female spy, one that goes snooping around.
  ēmissīcius, -a, -um, spying, prying (**ēmissārius, -ī**, *m*, an emissary, spy). Comic coinages.
42 *verberō**, (1), to lash, whip, beat.
43 **tē**: ablative with **dignam**. **mala**: "old." **malam aetātem**: "old age."
  exigō, exigere (3), **exēgī, exāctum**, to drive out, spend, pass (time).
44 *aedēs, aedis** (*f*), house (often plural for a single house).
45 *stimulus, -ī** (*m*), goad, spur, sting, whip. **seges, segetis** (*f*), corn field, crop.
46 *illūc**, to that place, there.
  regredior, regredī (3), **regressus sum**, to go back, withdraw, retire. **regredere**: imperative.
  ōstium, -ī (*n*), door. *sīs**: = **sī vīs**, "if you wish," "please."
47 **incēdō, incēdere** (3), **incessī**, to step, walk. *quōmodo**, how.
48 *fūstis, fūstis** (*m*), stick, club.
49 **testūdineus, -a, -um**, like a tortoise (**testūdō, testūdinis**, *f*).
  grandiō, grandīre (4), to make large (**grandis, -is, -e**), increase. Note the 4th conjugation future in **-bō**. *gradus, -ūs** (*m*), step, pace.
50 *utinam**: particle introducing a wish, expressed by the present subjunctive. *dīvus, -ī** (*m*), god.
  adigō, adigere (3), **adēgī, adāctum**, to drive to a place or thing. **suspendium, -ī** (*n*), hanging.
51 *pactum, -ī** (*n*), agreement, manner, way. *serviō** (4) (+ *dat.*), to serve, be a slave.
52 *scelestus, -a, -um**, cursed, wicked, villainous (a colloquial term of abuse).
  sēcum: = **cum sē**. **murmurō** (1), to mutter, murmur.
53 *improbus, -a, -um**, shameless, presumptuous, insolent.
  *effodiō, effodere** (3), **effōdī, effossum**, to dig up or out.

10

23	Huic fīlia ūna est. Ea mihi cotīdiē
24	aut tūre aut vīnō aut aliquī semper supplicat,
25	dat mihi corōnās. Eius honōris grātiā
26	fēcī thēsaurum ut hīc reperīret Eucliō,
27	quō illam facilius nūptum, sī vellet, daret,
28	Nam compressit eam dē summō adulēscēns locō.
29	Is scit adulēscēns quae sit quam compresserit,
30	illa illum nescit, neque compressam autem pater.
31	Eam ego hodiē faciam ut hīc senex dē proximō *(pointing to Megadorus' house)*
32	sibi uxōrem poscat. Id eā faciam grātiā
33	quō ille eam facilius dūcat quī compresserat.
34	Et hic quī poscet eam sibi uxōrem senex,
35	is adulēscentis illīus est avunculus,
36	quī illam stuprāvit noctū, Cereris vigiliīs.
	(Shouts are heard from Euclio's house.)
37	Sed hic senex iam clāmat intus ut solet.
38	Anum forās extrūdit, nē sit cōnscia.
39	Crēdō aurum īnspicere vult, nē surreptum sit.

Euclio (EUC.) *comes from his house shoving Staphyla* (STA.) *before him,*
scolding her and beating her with his stick. Invisible to Euclio and
Staphyla, the Lar dances into the house once they are out of the doorway.

40	EUC. *(to Staphyla)* Exī, inquam! Age exī! Exeundum hercle tibi hinc est forās,
41	circumspectātrix cum oculīs ēmissīciīs.
42	STA. Nam cūr mē miseram verberās? EUC. Ut misera sīs
43	atque ut tē dignam mala malam aetātem exigās.
44	STA. Nam quā mē nunc causā extrūsistī ex aedibus?
45	EUC. Tibi ego ratiōnem reddam, stimulōrum seges?
	(indicating a place well away from the house)
46	Illūc regredere ab ōstiō. *(aside to the audience)* Illūc sīs vidē,
47	ut incēdit. *(to Staphyla, who shuffles a few steps in the direction indicated)*
	At scīsne quōmodo tibi rēs sē habet? *(threatening her with his stick)*
48	Sī hercle hodiē fūstem cēperō aut stimulum in manum,
49	testūdineum istum tibi ego grandibō gradum.
50	STA. *(to herself)* Utinam mē dīvī adigant ad suspendium
51	potius quidem quam hōc pactō apud tē servem.
52	EUC. *(to himself)* At ut scelesta sōla sēcum murmurat!
53	*(shouting at Staphyla)* Oculōs hercle ego istōs, improba, effodiam tibi,
54	nē mē observāre possīs quid rērum geram.

1. **What does the daughter do for the Lar?** (23–25)
2. **Why does the Lar allow Euclio to find the treasure?** (27)
3. **What has happened to the daughter?** (28) **What does she not know?** (30) **What does Euclio not know?** (30)
4. **What is the Lar going to cause to happen?** (31–32) **Why?** (32–33)
5. **What is the relationship of the *senex* (31) to the young man?** (34–36)
6. **How does Euclio describe Staphyla?** (40–49) **What does she say of herself?** (42, 50–51)
7. **Why does Euclio want to blind Staphyla?** (54)

55 **abscēdō, abscēdere** (3), **abscessī, abscessum,** to go away, withdraw.
ohē, interjection used in calling on someone to stop.
56 *****istīc,** there, over there. *****astō, astāre** (1), **astitī,** to stand by, stand still. **astātō:** future imperative (translate as simple imperative).
*****istic, istaec, istuc** (**iste** + **-ce**), that (of yours). **istōc:** ablative singular.
57 **digitus, -ī** (*m*), finger, toe. **trānsversus, -a, -um,** turned across, crosswise. **digitum trānsversum:** accusative of extent of space, "a finger across," "a finger's breadth."
*****unguis, unguis** (*m*), fingernail, toenail.
lātus, -a, -um, broad, wide. **excēdō, excēdere** (3), **excessī, excessum,** to go away, depart.
58 *****respiciō, respicere** (3), **respexī, respectum,** to look back. **dōnicum** (**dōnec**), until, before.
59 *****continuō** (*adv.*), immediately. **discipula, -ae** (*f*), female pupil.
*****crux, crucis** (*f*), cross (on which criminals were exposed to die), plague, torment.
60 **Scelestiōrem** (**anum**) **mē:** object and subject, respectively, of **vidēre** (61). *****certō,** certainly.
61 *****nimis,** too much, too, very. *****metuō, metuere** (2), **metuī, metūtum,** to fear. Verbs of fearing are followed by clauses introduced by **nē** for a thing one fears will happen.
*****male,** badly, severely. Note the alliteration.
62 *****verbum, -ī** (*n*), word. **verba dare alicui,** to give someone empty words, deceive, cheat. **imprūdēns, imprūdentis,** unaware, incautious.
63 **neu:** = **nēve** (**nē** + **-ve**), "or that." **persentīscō, persentīscere** (3), to become aware of.
abscondō, abscondere (3), **abscondī, absconditum,** to conceal from view, hide. **est absconditum:** note the colloquial use of the indicative in an indirect question.
64 **occipitium, -ī** (*n*), the back of the head (**ob-** + **caput**).
65 **vīsō, vīsere** (4), **vīsī, vīsum,** to look at. **-ne** (*in indirect questions*), whether, if. **estne:** note the colloquial use of the indicative in an indirect question.
*****condō, condere** (3), **condidī, conditum,** to put away, keep safe, bury, hide.
66 *****sollicitō** (1), to disturb, trouble, worry. *****plūrimus, -a, -um,** most, (plural) very many.
67 **noenum** (*adv.*), an archaic equivalent of **nōn.** The negative goes with **queō commīnīscī** (69) to make up the basic sentence.
*****mecastor,** by Castor! (= **mē Castor adiuvet;** a woman's oath). Castor and his brother Pollux were regarded as gods able to protect sailors in storms. *****erus, -ī** (*m*), master.
68 **malae reī:** partitive genitive with **quid** (67).
*****ēveniō, ēvenīre** (4), **ēvēnī, ēventum** (+ *dat.*), to happen to. **-ve,** or. **īnsania, -ae** (*f*), madness.
69 *****queō, quīre** (*irreg.*), **quīvī** or **quiī,** to be able.
*****commīnīscor, commīnīscī** (3), **commentus sum,** to think up.
70 **deciēns,** ten times.
71 *****pol,** by Pollux! *****illic, illaec, illuc** (**ille** + **-ce**), that, **illunc:** masc. acc. sing.
intemperiae, -ārum (*f pl*), lack of temperateness, immoderateness, insanity.
tenent: note the colloquial use of the indicative in an indirect question.
72 **pervigilō** (1), to stay awake all night. **interdius** (*adv.*), in the daytime.
73 *****quasi,** as, as if, just like. **claudus, -a, -um,** lame, limping, crippled.
*****sūtor, sūtōris** (*m*), shoemaker, cobbler.
74 *****cēlō** (1), to hide. *****erīlis, -is, -e,** of or belonging to a master (**erus, -ī,** *m*).
75 *****probrum, -ī** (*n*), disgrace, scandal. *****partitūdō, partitūdinis** (*f*), the act of giving birth.
appetō, appetere (3), **appetīvī** or **appetiī, appetītum** (+ *dat.*), to be near, approach.
76 **melius . . . quam** (77): followed by **ut** and the subjunctive.
77 *****opīnor, opīnārī** (1), **opīnātus sum,** to think, believe. **ūnam . . . litteram:** i.e., the letter *I.*
78 **laqueus, -ī** (*m*), noose. **collum, -ī** (*n*), neck. *****quandō,** when.
obstringō, obstringere (3), **obstrīnxī, obstrīctum,** to bind.
79 **dēfaecō,** (1), to remove the dregs (**faex, faecis,** *f*) from, strain, clear.
dēmum, at last. **ēgredior, ēgredī** (3), **ēgressus sum,** to go or come out.
80 *****salvus, -a, -um,** safe, secure, unharmed.
81 *****nunciam,** this instant, here and now. *****intrō,** inside (with verbs implying motion).
quippinī, why not? of course! naturally!
82 **servem:** what use of the subjunctive?
An: need not be translated here; simply introduces the second of two questions.
*****aedīs:** = **aedēs.** *****auferō, auferre** (*irreg.*), **abstulī, ablātum,** to carry away, steal.
83 **quaestus, -ī** (*usually* **-ūs**) (*m*), income, profit. **quaestī:** partitive genitive with **nihil.**
*****fūr, fūris** (*m*), thief.
84 **ināniae, -ārum** (*f pl*), emptiness, nothingness. **opplētus, -a, -um** (+ *abl.*), filled with.
*****arānea, -ae** (*f*), cobweb.

12

(as Staphyla moves farther away from the house)

55 Abscēde etiam nunc—etiam nunc—etiam—ohē,
56 istīc astātō. Sī hercle tū ex istōc locō
57 digitum trānsversum aut unguem lātum excesseris
58 aut sī respexeris, dōnicum ego tē iusserō,
59 continuō hercle ego tē dēdam discipulam crucī.
60 *(aside to the audience)* Scelestiōrem mē hāc anū certō sciō
61 vīdisse numquam, nimisque ego hanc metuō male
62 nē mī ex īnsidiīs verba imprūdentī det
63 neu persentīscat aurum ubi est absconditum,
64 quae in occipitiō quoque habet oculōs pessima.

(turning toward his house, still aside to the audience)

65 Nunc ībo ut vīsam, estne ita aurum ut condidī,
66 quod mē sollicitat plūrimīs miserum modīs.

(Euclio goes back into his house.)

67 **STA.** *(alone, to herself)* Noenum mecastor quid ego erō dīcam meō
68 malae reī ēvēnisse quamve īnsāniam
69 queō comminīscī; ita mē miseram ad hunc modum
70 deciēns diē ūnō saepe extrūdit aedibus.
71 Nesciō pol quae illunc hominem intemperiae tenent:
72 pervigilat noctēs tōtās, tum autem interdius
73 quasi claudus sūtor domī sedet tōtōs diēs.
74 *(pensive)* Neque iam quō pactō celem erīlis fīliae
75 probrum, propinqua partitūdō cui appetit,
76 queō comminīscī; neque quicquam melius est mihi,
77 ut opīnor, quam ex mē ut ūnam faciam litteram
78 longam, meum laqueō collum quandō obstrīnxerō. *(She imitates a hanging corpse.)*

EUC. *(returning, reassured and confident; to himself)*

79 Nunc dēfaecātō dēmum animō ēgredior domō,
80 postquam perspexī salva esse intus omnia.
81 *(to Staphyla)* Redī nunciam intrō atque intus servā. **STA.** Quippinī?
82 Ego intus servem? An nē quis aedīs auferat?
83 Nam hīc apud nōs nihil est aliud quaestī fūribus,
84 ita ināniīs sunt opplētae atque arāneīs.

1. What does Euclio say he will do to Staphyla if she moves? (59)
2. What is Euclio worried that Staphyla might do? (62–63)
3. Why does Euclio depart at the end of his speech? (65–66)
4. What does Staphyla think of Euclio? (67–69) What does he do to her? (69–70)
5. What does Euclio do at night? (72) During the day? (72–73)
6. What is Staphyla worried about? (74–76) What does she think of doing? (76–78)
7. In what frame of mind does Euclio return? (79)
8. What does he order Staphyla to do? (81) How does she react? (81–84)

85 **mīrus, -a, -um**, remarkable. **Mīrum quīn** (+ *subjunctive*): "It is a wonder that . . . not."
　tuā . . . causā, for your sake.
86 ***Philippus, -ī** (*m*), Philip II, king of Macedonia and father of Alexander the Great.
　Dārēus (Dārīus), -ī (*m*), Darius, king of Persia, defeated by Alexander.
　trivenēfica, -ae (*f*), triple poison-mixer, thorough witch, hag. A comic coinage.
88 ***pauper, pauperis**, poor. ***fateor, fatērī** (2), **fassus sum**, to admit. ***dī**: = **deī**.
89 ***occlūdō, occlūdere** (3), **occlūsī, occlūsum**, to close, shut (a door). **iam**, soon.
90 **Cavē . . . mīserīs**: perfect subjunctive in a prohibition, "Watch out that you don't. . . ."
91 **quod**: here "in case," "if" (with present subjunctive, **quaerat**, "should seek"). **quis-piam, quaepiam, quippiam (quidpiam)**, someone, something.
92 **causae**: partitive genitive with **quid** (= **aliquid**). **causae quid sit quod**: "there be any reason why. . . . " + present subjunctive. **quaeritō** (1), to ask a person for something.
93 **exstinguēre**: = **exstinguēris**, "you will be extinguished." ***extemplō**, at once, immediately.
94 **aufugiō, aufugere** (3), **aufūgī**, to run away, disappear, vanish. ***dīcitō**: future imperative.
95 ***culter, cultrī** (*m*), knife. **secūris, secūris** (*f*), ax, hatchet. **pistillus, -ī** (*m*), pestle.
　mortārium, -ī (*n*), mortar.
96 **ūtenda . . . rogant**: "they ask to borrow." ***vās, vāsis; (*pl*) vāsa, -ōrum** (*n*), dish, utensil.
　***vīcīnus, -ī** (*m*), neighbor.
97 **abstulisse**: from **auferō**.
98 ***profectō** (*adv.*), without question, assuredly, absolutely.
99 ***praedicō** (1), to proclaim, declare.
100 **Bona Fortūna**: the goddess of good fortune, worshiped with various cult titles.
　mīserīs: perfect subjunctive in a prohibition.
102 **quāquam**, in any way, by any means.
103 ***taceō, tacēre** (2), **tacuī, tacitum**, to be silent. **sīs**: = **sī vīs** (see line 46).
104 ***foris, foris** (*f*), door, (plural) double door or its two leaves.
　ambōbus: i.e., the upper and lower **pessulī**. **pessulus, -ī** (*m*), bolt of a door.
105 **discruciō** (1), to torture, torment. **animī**: locative of the location of the torment.
107 ***magister, magistrī** (*m*), master, manager, official.
　cūria, -ae (*f*), one of the thirty divisions of the Roman people established by Romulus, by which voting took place in the **comitia cūriāta**, the assembly of the Roman people for the election of magistrates.
108 **dīvidere**: present infinitive where we would expect a future, "that he would divide." ***argentum, -ī** (*n*), silver, money.
　***nummus, -ī** (*m*), coin, the silver didrachm used in the Greek cities of southern Italy.
　in virōs: = **viritim**, to each man separately.
109 ***ac**, and. **īlicō**, on the spot, just there, immediately.
110 **suspicentur**: potential subjunctive, here with the sense of the future indicative.
112 **pauxillum, -ī** (*n*), a small quantity, a little. **parvī facere**: genitive of value, "to regard as of small value."
　quīn (+ *subjunctive*), so as not to. **nummōrum**: partitive genitive with **pauxillum**.
113 **cēlō**: see line 74. Here the verb means "to exclude from knowledge," "refrain from informing," "keep in ignorance," and is followed by **omnīs** as its direct object.
　sēdulō (*adv.*), with care, diligently, zealously.
114 ***benignē**, in a friendly spirit, kindly, profusely.
115 ***salūtō** (1), to greet. ***prius**, formerly, before.
116 **copulor, copulārī** (1), **copulātus sum**, to join.
117 ***rogitō** (1), to ask frequently or insistently. **ut**: here, "whether."
118 **postideā**, afterwards.
119 **quantum poterō**, as quickly as I can. **tantum**, so quickly.
　***sē recipere**, to take oneself back, return.

85 EUC. Mīrum quīn tuā mē causā faciat Iuppiter
86 Philippum rēgem aut Dārēum, trivenēfica.
87 *(angry and threatening)* Arāneās mī ego illās servārī volō.
88 Pauper sum; fateor, patior; quod dī dant ferō.
89 Abī intrō, occlūde iānuam. *(turning as if about to leave, then threaten-*
    ingly to Staphyla) Iam ego hīc erō.
90 Cavē quemquam aliēnum in aedīs intrō mīseris.
91 Quod quispiam ignem quaerat, exstinguī volō,
92 nē causae quid sit quod tē quisquam quaeritet.
93 Nam sī ignis vīvet, tū exstinguere extemplō.
94 Tum aquam aufūgisse dīcitō, sī quis petet.
95 Cultrum, secūrim, pistillum, mortārium,
96 quae ūtenda vāsa semper vīcīnī rogant,
97 fūrēs vēnisse atque abstulisse dīcitō.
98 Profectō in aedīs meās mē absente nēminem
99 volō intrō mittī. *(adding one last order)* Atque etiam hoc praedicō tibi,
100 sī Bona Fortūna veniat, nē intrō mīseris.
101 STA. Pol ea ipsa crēdō nē intrō mittātur cavet,
102 nam ad aedīs nostrās numquam adiit quāquam prope.
103 EUC. Tacē atque abī intrō. *(Staphyla goes back into the house as Euclio gives*
    his final instructions.) STA. Taceō atque abeō. EUC. Occlūde sīs
104 forēs ambōbus pessulīs. Iam ego hīc erō. *(alone; worriedly to himself)*
105 Discrucior animī, quia ab domō abeundum est mihi.
106 Nimis hercle invītus abeō. Sed quid agam sciō.
107 Nam noster nostrae quī est magister cūriae
108 dīvidere argentī dīxit nummōs in virōs;
109 id sī relinquō ac nōn petō, omnēs īlicō
110 mē suspicentur, crēdō, habēre aurum domī.
111 Nam vērī simile nōn est hominem pauperem
112 pauxillum parvī facere quīn nummōrum petat.
113 Nam nunc cum cēlō sēdulō omnīs, nē sciant,
114 omnēs videntur scīre et mē benignius
115 omnēs salūtant quam salūtābant prius;
116 adeunt, cōnsistunt, cōpulantur dexterās,
117 rogitant mē ut valeam, quid agam, quid rērum geram.
    (finally hurrying off to the audience's right)
118 Nunc quō profectus sum ībō; postideā domum
119 mē rūrsus quantum poterō tantum recipiam.

1. **Why would Euclio think of a comparison between himself and Philip or Darius?** (86)
2. **How does Euclio describe himself in line 88? Is this true?**
3. **Why does Euclio want Staphyla to put out the fire?** (92)
4. **What is Staphyla to tell anyone who asks to borrow anything?** (97)
5. **How does Euclio feel about leaving the house?** (105–106)
6. **Where is he going?** (107–108) **Why does he feel he must go?** (109–112)
7. **What has Euclio noticed about the behavior of his acquaintances?** (113–117)

120 **Velim**: potential subjunctive.
122 *__aequus__, -a, -um, level, equal, right. **aequum est** (+ *acc. and infinitive*), it is right that or for. With **germānam sorōrem** supply **facere**.
  germānus, -a, -um, having the same father and mother, full (of brothers and sisters).
123 *__haud__, not.
  *__fallō__, **fallere** (3), **fefellī**, **falsum**, to trick, mislead, (passive) to be in error, be under an illusion. **nōs**: supply **fēminās**.
  odiōsus, -a, -um, disagreeable, offensive, tiresome, annoying. **habērī**: "to be considered."
124 **multum**, very. **loquāx**, **loquācis**, talkative, loquacious. *__meritō__, deservedly.
125 **nec . . . nūllam**: = **nec . . . ūllam**.
  mūtus, -a, -um, that can only mutter, speechless, dumb.
126 **saeculum**, -ī (*n*), age, generation, century.
127 *__vērum__, but truly. **cōgitātō**: future imperative.
128 **proximus**, -a, -um, nearest.
129 *__in rem esse__: "to be of advantage," "to be in one's interest."
  utrīusque (*gen.*): "of both of us."
130 **mihi . . . tibi**: datives with **cōnsulere**, (here) "to consult the interests of," "to look after."
131 **occultum . . . habērī**: "to be kept hidden." **per** (+ *acc.*), because of.
  mussō (1), to mutter, keep quiet. **mussārī**: = **tacērī**.
132 **quīn**: here introducing a result clause; supply **faciam**: "without my making you. . . ."
  particeps, **participis** (*m*), participant, sharer. **pariter**, equally.
133 *__eō__, for this reason. **sēcrētō**, separately, individually, in private.
  sēdūcō, **sēdūcere** (3), **sēdūxī**, **sēductum**, to draw (a person) aside.
134 *__tēcum__: = **cum tē**.
136 **quis . . . nam**: = **quisnam**, **quaenam**, **quidnam**, who? what? Here **quis . . . nam** is feminine.
137 *__aiō__, **ais**, **ait**, **aiunt**, to say yes, to say so. **ais**: pronounced as one syllable.
  Sī negās, negō: like our "If you don't want me to say it, I won't."
138 *__decet__, **decēre** (2), **decuit** (*impersonal*), it is becoming, right, fitting.
  *__equidem__, indeed, in truth.
  *__prōloquor__, **prōloquī** (3), **prōlocūtus sum**, to speak forth.
139 **ēligō**, **ēligere** (3), **ēlēgī**, **ēlēctum**, to pull out, select, choose.
141 **adversor**, **adversārī** (1), **adversātus sum** (+ *dat.*), to oppose (in argument).
  certus, -a, -um, fixed, certain, sure. *__certum est__: "my mind is made up," "I am certain."
142 *__operam dare__ (+ *dat.*), to pay attention to.
142a **amābō**: "please." **Tua est**: "My attention is yours." **ūtere**: imperative of **ūtor**.
143 *__quid__: = **aliquid** (after **sī**).
145 **monitum**: supine expressing purpose. **adventō** (1), to come toward, approach.
146 **mōre tuō**: ablative of manner, "in your usual way."
  facta volō: = **haec fierī volō**, "I want (to see) that these things get done."
147 **sempiternus**, -a, -um, lasting forever, permanent.
148 **salūtāris**, -is, -e, promoting one's safety or well-being (**salūs**, **salūtis**, *f*), wholesome, beneficial.
  prōcreō (1), to engender, beget (children). **līberīs prōcreandīs**: dative of purpose to be taken with the rest of Eunomia's sentence in lines 149–150.
149 **faciant**: subjunctive in a wish.
150 *__ei__ (*pronounced as a single syllable*), alas!
  *__occidō__, **occidere** (3), **occidī**, **occāsum**, to fall or collapse in the way, die, be done for, be ruined.

As Euclio departs to the right to go to the forum, the stage is left empty for a few moments. Then Eunomia (EUN.) and Megadorus (MEG.) enter from the latter's house on the right, engaging initially in a light and affectionately bantering song.

120 EUN. *(to Megadorus)* Velim tē arbitrārī mē haec verba, frāter,
121   meae fideī tuaeque reī   SONG
122   causā facere, ut aequum est germānam sorōrem.
123   Quamquam haud falsa sum nōs odiōsās habērī;
124   nam multum loquācēs meritō omnēs habēmur,
125   nec mūtam profectō repertam nūllam esse
126   aut hodiē dīcunt mulierem aut ūllō in saeculō.
127   Vērum hoc, frāter, ūnum tamen cōgitātō,
128   tibi proximam mē mihique esse item tē;
129   ita aequum est quod in rem esse utrīusque arbitrēmur
130   et mihi tē et tibi mē cōnsulere et monēre;
131   neque occultum id habērī neque per metum mussārī
132   quīn participem pariter ego tē et tū mē faciās.
133   Eō nunc ego sēcrētō tē hūc forās sēdūxī,
134   ut tuam rem ego tēcum hīc loquerer familiārem.
135 MEG. *(extending his hand to Eunomia)* Dā mī, optima fēmina, manum.
136 EUN. *(pretending to look around)* Ubi ea est? Quis ea est nam optima?
137 MEG. Tū. EUN. Tūne ais? MEG. Sī negās, negō.
138 EUN. Decet tē equidem vēra prōloquī;
139   nam optima nūlla potest ēligī:
140   alia aliā pēior, frāter, est. MEG. Idem ego arbitror,
141   nec tibi adversārī certum est dē istāc rē umquam, soror.
142 EUN. Dā mihi
142a   operam amābō. MEG. Tua est, ūtere atque
143   imperā, sī quid vīs.
144 EUN. Id quod in rem tuam optimum esse arbitror,
145   tē id monitum adventō.
146 MEG. Soror, mōre tuō facis. EUN. Facta volō.
147 MEG. Quid est id, soror? EUN. Quod tibi sempiternum
148   salūtāre sit: līberīs prōcreandīs—
149 MEG. *(interrupting Eunomia)* Ita dī faciant— EUN. *(resuming her sentence)*
       Volō tē uxōrem
150   domum dūcere. MEG. *(wincing as if he had received a blow to the head)*
       Ei occidī! EUN. Quid ita?

1. **How does Eunomia hope her brother will regard her approach to him?** (120–122)
2. **What do people usually think of women?** (123–126)
3. **Why does Eunomia feel it is within her domain to advise her brother?** (127–132)
4. **What does Megadorus call Eunomia?** (135) **How does Eunomia respond?** (136–140)
5. **Is Megadorus argumentative with Eunomia?** (140–141)
6. **How does Eunomia feel about what she is going to advise?** (144–145)
7. **What does she advise and why?** (147–150) **How does Megadorus react?** (150)

151 **cerebrum, -ī** (*n*), brain. **excutiō, excutere** (3), **excussī, excussum**, to knock out.
152 **dictum, -ī** (*n*), that which is said, (plural) one's words.
153 *****heia** (*an interjection expressing urgency; pronounced as two syllables*), come on!
   *****libet, libēre** (2), **libuit** or **libitum est** (*impersonal*), it is pleasing, agreeable. Supply
     mihi. What kind of a conditional sentence is this?
154 *****ut**: = **utinam** (with subjunctive of wish). **ēmorior, ēmorī** (3), **ēmortuus sum**, to
     perish, die.
   dūcam: supply **fēminam in mātrimōnium**. Why is the subjunctive used here?
155 **quam**: = **aliquam** (after **sī**).
156 **perendiē**, on the day after tomorrow. **ferātur** (*jussive subjunctive*): i.e., out for
     burial.
157 *****cedo** (*imperative*), give! hand over! bring!
   *****nūptiae, -ārum** (*f pl*), marriage ceremony and festivities, wedding.
   adornō (1), to get ready, prepare.
158 **possum tibi . . . dare**: supply **fēminam aliquam**. *****dōs, dōtis** (*f*), dowry.
159 *****grandis, -is, -e**, grown up, old.
   nātū (*abl. sing. supine of* **nascor, nascī**, 3, **nātus sum**, to be born), with respect to
     birth, in age.
161 **Num nōn**: note the implied double negative in Megadorus' hesitant question.
   interrogō (1), to ask.
   *****immō** (*introducing the correction of a previous statement or question*), rather, on
     the contrary.
162 **mediā**: ablative of description with **aetāte** understood, "of middle age."
163 **praegnās, praegnātis**, pregnant. **fortuitō**, by chance.
164 **quīn**: the verb **dubitāre** may be followed by **quīn**, "that," and the subjunctive.
   Postumus, -ī (*m*), a proper name (from the adjective **postumus, -a, -um**, last-born,
     born after the father's death).
165 *****dēmō, dēmere** (3), **dēmpsī, dēmptum**, to remove, take away, cut off.
   dēminuō, dēminuere (3), **dēminuī, dēminūtum**, to lessen.
166 **virtūte deōrum**: "thanks to the gods." **maiōrēs, maiōrum** (*m pl*), ancestors.
   *****dīves, dīvitis**, wealthy, rich.
167 **factiō, factiōnis** (*f*), the act of making or producing, political faction, social connec-
     tions.
   animōs: here, "haughty feelings," "pride," "airs."
   dapsilis, -is, -e (*Greek loan word*), plentiful, abundant. **dapsilīs**: = **dapsilēs**.
168 **eborātus, -a, -um**, adorned with ivory (**ebur, eboris**, *n*).
   *****vehiculum, -ī** (*n*), carriage.
   palla, -ae (*f*), a rectangular mantle (worn as an outdoor garment by women).
   *****purpura, -ae** (*f*), purple-dyed clothing.
169 *****nīl**: = **nihil. moror, morārī** (1), **morātus sum**, to delay. **nīl moror**: "I don't care for,"
     "I don't much like." *****sūmptus, -ūs** (*m*), expense, cost, charge.
   redigō, redigere (3), **redēgī, redāctum**, to drive or send back, reduce.
170 *****audeō, audēre** (2), **ausus sum**, to have a mind (to do something), be prepared, in-
     tend, dare. **sī audēs**: "if you please."
171 **pauperculus, -a, -um** (*diminutive expressing commiseration*), poor.
173 *****virgō, virginis**, unwedded, (as a noun) unwedded woman.
   *****dēspondeō, dēspondēre** (3), **dēspondī, dēspōnsum**, to promise (a woman) in mar-
     riage, betroth.
   Verba nē faciās: "Don't interrupt."
174 **es**: colloquial use of the indicative in an indirect question.
175 **bene vertant**: jussive subjunctive, "make (the matter) turn out well."
176 *****conveniō, convenīre** (4), **convēnī, conventum**, to come together, visit.
177 *****eccum**: = **ecce eum**, here he is!
   Nesciō unde: "I don't know from where," "From some place or other."

151   **MEG.** Quia mī miserō cerebrum excutiunt
152   tua dicta, soror: lapidēs loqueris.
153   **EUN.** Heia, hoc fac quod tē iubet soror. **MEG.** Sī libeat, faciam.
154   **EUN.** In rem hoc tuam est. **MEG.** Ut quidem ēmoriar priusquam dūcam.
155   Sed hīs lēgibus sī quam dare vīs, dūcam:
156   quae crās veniat, perendiē, soror, forās ferātur;
157   hīs lēgibus quam dare vīs? Cedo: nūptiās adornā.
158   **EUN.** *(ignoring Megadorus' witticism)* Cum maximā possum tibi, frāter, dare dōte;
159   sed est grandior nātū: media est mulieris aetās.
160   Eam sī iubēs, frāter, tibi mē poscere, poscam.
161   **MEG.** Num nōn vīs mē interrogāre tē? **EUN.** Immō, sī quid vīs, rogā. RECITATIVE
162   **MEG.** Post mediam aetātem quī mediā dūcit uxōrem domum,
163   sī eam senex anum praegnātem fortuitō fēcerit,
164   quid dubitās quīn sit parātum nōmen puerō Postumus?
165   Nunc ego istum, soror, labōrem dēmam et dēminuam tibi.
166   Ego virtūte deōrum et maiōrum nostrōrum dīves sum satis.
167   Istās magnās factiōnēs, animōs, dōtēs dapsilīs,
168   clāmōrēs, imperia, eborāta vehicula, pallās, purpuram
169   nīl moror, quae in servitūtem sūmptibus redigunt virōs.
170   **EUN.** Dīc mihi, sī audēs, quis ea est quam vīs dūcere uxōrem? **MEG.** *(dropping his playful tone and smugly making his own proposal)* Ēloquar.
171   Nōvistīne hunc senem Euclıōnem ex proximō pauperculum?
172   **EUN.** Nōvī, hominem haud malum mecastor. **MEG.** Eius cupiō fīliam
173   virginem mī dēspondērī. *(Eunomia winces with disbelief and is about to object; Megadorus restrains her.)* Verba nē faciās, soror.
174   Sciō quid dictūra es: hanc esse pauperem. Haec pauper placet.
175   **EUN.** *(with resignation)* Dī bene vertant. **MEG.** Idem ego spērō. **EUN.** *(about to depart)* Quid mē? Num quid vīs? **MEG.** Valē.
176   **EUN.** *(as she departs off stage to the right, toward her home)* Et tū, frāter. **MEG.** *(alone, to himself, as he goes toward Euclio's house)* Ego conveniam Euclıōnem, sī domī est.

Euclio, returning from the forum, enters from the right in a bad mood, grumbling to himself and not seeing Megadorus.

177   **MEG.** *(noticing Euclio)* Sed eccum videō. Nesciō unde sēsē homō recipit domum.

1.   **Does Eunomia accept Megadorus' reaction to her suggestion?** (151–153)
2.   **What are Megadorus' conditions for following Eunomia's suggestion?** (155–157)
3.   **What kind of a woman does Eunomia have in mind for Megadorus?** (158–160)
4.   **Why does Megadorus not want to marry a middle-aged woman?** (162–164)
5.   **What reason does Megadorus give in line 166 for not wanting to marry a woman with a large dowry?**
6.   **What does Megadorus fear that a wife with a large dowry would bring with her?** (167–168) **How would this affect Megadorus?** (169)
7.   **What does Eunomia think of Euclio?** (172)
8.   **Why might Eunomia object to Megadorus' choice for a wife?** (174)

178 **praesāgiō** (4), to have a foreboding.
    īre: present infinitive for future, "that I would go."
179 **itaque**, and so. **cūriālis, cūriālis** (m), a member of the same **cūria** (see line 107).
181 ***properō** (1), to hurry, do, get ready with haste.
182 ***fortūnātus, -a, -um**, successful, prosperous, lucky, wealthy.
183 ***rēctē**, rightly, well. **rēctē valēre**, to be in good health, be well.
184 **temerārius, -a, -um**, accidental, by chance.
    *blandē, cordially, in a fawning manner.
186 **perbene**, very well. **ā pecūniā**: "as to my financial circumstances."
187 ***quī** (*old form of ablative, here introducing a purpose clause*), in order that by this
    means.
188 ***indicium, -ī** (n), disclosure (of a fact), information. **indicium facere**, to give away a
    secret.
    perspicuē, clearly.
    *palam, openly, publicly. **palam esse**, to be generally known, be common knowledge.
189 **lingua, -ae** (f), tongue.
    praecīdo, praecīdere (3), **praecīdī, praecīsum**, to cut the tip off, cut back, lop off.
190 **loquere**: = **loqueris**. ***pauperiēs, pauperiēī** (f), poverty.
    *conqueror, conquerī (3), **conquestus sum**, to lament, complain of.
191 **virginem . . . grandem**: "a full-grown girl."
    cassus, -a, -um (+ *abl.*), devoid of, lacking.
    illocābilis, -is, -e, that cannot be contracted out in marriage.
192 ***locō** (1), to put, place, give a girl in marriage to someone.
193 **dabitur**: supply **dōs** or **pecūnia** as subject.
    adiūvō, adiūvāre (1), **adiūvī, adiūtum**, to help. **adiūvābere**: = **adiūvāberis**.
    *opus est (+ *acc.* or *abl.*), there is need of.
194 ***inhiō** (1), to open one's mouth (for food), gape after. **dēvorō** (1), to gulp down.
195 **ostentō** (1), to hold up, present. Euclio quotes a proverb about luring a dog with
    food in order to kill it.
196 **largē**, generously, liberally.
    blandus, -a, -um, courteous, ingratiating, fawning upon (+ dative).
    dīves: in apposition to the relative pronoun, "who, as a rich man, is. . . . "
197 **iniciō, inicere** (3), **iniēcī, iniectum**, to throw in or on. **onerō** (1), to load, heap on.
    *aliquī, aliqua (or **aliquae**), **aliquod**, some. **zāmia, -ae** (f) (*Greek loan word*), hurt,
    damage, loss.
198 **pōlypus, -ī** (m) (*Greek loan word*), octopus. ***quisquis, quidquid** (**quicquid**), whoever,
    whatever.
199 **parumper**, for a short while, for a moment. **operae est**: "(you) can spare the effort."
200 **appellāre**, (here) to appeal to someone (**tē**) for or about something (**quod**).
201 **harpagō** (1) (*Greek loan word*), to steal, carry off. In Molière's *L'Avare*, adapted from
    this play of Plautus, the miser is named Harpagon.
202 ***mēcum**: = **cum mē**. **mēcum . . . pactiōnem**: in apposition to **eam rem** (201).
    pactiō, pactiōnis (f), agreement, terms.
    *intervīsō, intervīsere (3), **intervīsī, intervīsum**, to go and see.
203 **revertor, revertī** (3), **reversus sum**, to return, come back.
    quod: the antecedent, "something," is omitted.
    invīsō, invīsere (3), **invīsī, invīsum**, to go to see.

know commentary

EUC. *(to himself, still not seeing Megadorus)*

178 Praesāgiēbat mī animus frūstrā mē īre, cum exībam domō;

179 itaque abībam invītus; nam neque quisquam cūriālium

180 vēnit neque magister quem dīvidere argentum oportuit.

181 Nunc domum properāre properō, nam ego sum hīc, animus domī est.

MEG. *(going up to Euclio to greet him cordially)*

182 Salvus atque fortūnātus, Eucliō, semper sīs.

183 EUC. *(politely)* Dī tē ament, Megadōre. MEG. Quid tū? Rēctēne atque ut vīs valēs?

184 EUC. *(aside)* Nōn temerārium est ubi dīves blandē appellat pauperem.

185 Iam illic homō aurum scit mē habēre, eō mē salūtat blandius.

MEG. *(with continuing genial good humor)*

186 Aisne tū tē valēre? EUC. Pol ego haud perbene ā pecūniā.

187 MEG. Pol sī est animus aequus tibi, satis habēs quī bene vītam colās.

188 EUC. *(aside in alarm)* Anus hercle huic indicium fēcit dē aurō, perspicuē palam est,

189 cui ego iam linguam praecīdam atque oculōs effodiam domī.

190 MEG. *(baffled)* Quid tū sōlus tēcum loquere? EUC. *(startled into inventing a plausible excuse)* Meam pauperiem conqueror.

191 virginem habeō grandem, dōte cassam atque illocābilem,

192 neque eam queō locāre cuiquam. MEG. *(affably)* Tacē, bonum habē animum, Eucliō.

193 Dabitur, adiuvābere ā mē. Dīc, sī quid opus est, imperā.

194 EUC. *(aside, worried)* Nunc petit, cum pollicētur; inhiat aurum ut dēvoret.

195 Alterā manū fert lapidem, pānem ostentat alterā.

196 Nēminī crēdō quī largē blandus est dīves pauperī:

197 ubi manum inicit benignē, ibi onerat aliquam zāmiam.

198 Ego istōs nōvī polypōs, quī ubi quidquid tetigērunt tenent.

(Euclio prepares to pass Megadorus and go to his own house.)

199 MEG. *(blocking his path)* Da mī operam parumper, sī operae est, Eucliō, id quod tē volō

200 dē commūnī rē appellāre meā et tuā. EUC. *(aside)* Ei miserō mihi,

201 aurum mī intus harpagātum est. Nunc hic eam rem volt, sciō,

202 mēcum adīre ad pactiōnem. *(edging toward his house)* Vērum intervīsam domum.

203 MEG. Quō abīs? EUC. *(darting quickly into his house)* Iam revertar ad tē: nam est quod invīsam domum.

1. **Was Euclio's excursion from home worthwhile?** (178–180)
2. **Why does Euclio think that Megadorus greets him so pleasantly?** (184–185)
3. **What does Euclio say to Megadorus about his own monetary situation?** (186)
4. **What does Megadorus say is enough for a good life?** (187)
5. **What suspicion does Megadorus' comment arouse in Euclio?** (188)
6. **About what does Euclio complain?** (190–192)
7. **How does Megadorus propose to help?** (193)
8. **What does Euclio think Megadorus' real intentions are?** (194–195)
9. **What suspicion does Euclio have about wealthy men who befriend the poor?** (196–198)
10. **In what manner does Megadorus try to speak with Euclio?** (199–200)
11. **What does Euclio think is the reason Megadorus wishes to speak with him?** (200–202)
12. **What does Euclio do as a result?** (202–203)

204 *edepol, by Pollux!   *mentiō, mentiōnis (f), mention.
205 ut dēspondeat: indirect command or substantive clause of purpose after mentiōnem
    . . . fēcerō (204).
    *dērīdeō, dērīdēre (2), dērīsī, dērīsum, to laugh at, make fun of.
    reor, rērī (2), ratus sum, to think, imagine, suppose.
206 paupertās, paupertātis (f), poverty. ex paupertāte: "from the ranks of the poor."
    *parcus, -a, -um, thrifty, stingy.
208 exanimātus, -a, -um, lifeless, dead, faint with fear.
210 *quaesō, quaesere (3), to try to obtain, seek, (here) "I ask you," "please."
    *percontor, percontārī (1), percontātus sum, to question.
    piget, pigēre (2), piguit (impersonal), to affect with revulsion or displeasure, irk.
        Subjunctive of wish: "may it not. . . . "
211 dum . . . nē (+ present subjunctive): "provided you don't." libeat: supply mihi.
212 *quālis, -is, -e, of what kind, quality, or sort? arbitrāre: = arbitrāris.
    prōgnātus, -a, -um, born from.
213 quid fidē: = quālī fidē. quid factīs: = quālibus factīs. *factum, -ī (n), action, deed.
215 omnī: = ūllā. malitia, -ae (f), vice, fault.
216 oleō, olēre (2), oluī, to smell, give off a smell to someone (dative) so as to reveal
        one's presence to that person.
218 quae rēs: i.e., the betrothal to be requested in the following line.   *rēctē, rightly,
        well.
219 prōmittō, prōmittere (3), prōmīsī, prōmissum, to promise. fore: = futūrum esse.
220 decōrus, -a, -um, becoming, honorable, decent, in keeping with (+ ablative).
    *facinus, facinoris (n), deed, act. facinus . . . factīs facis: note the alliteration.
221 inops, inopis, lacking wealth, poor.
    innoxius, -a, -um, innocent, blameless. ab tē: "in relation to you."
    *irrīdeō, irrīdēre (2), irrīsī, irrīsum, to laugh at, mock.
223 dērīsum: supine expressing purpose.
224 *nāta, -ae (f), daughter.
227 factiōsus, -a, -um, busy, active, having a large following or many connections (cf.
    factiō, factiōnis, f, line 167). pauperum: genitive plural.
228 locāverim: the perfect subjunctive is used in the protasis of a future less vivid con-
    ditional sentence when the conditional act is regarded as having been completed
    ("if I should have . . .") before that of the apodosis begins. Here the condition is
    mixed, with the present indicative in the apodosis. The future less vivid construc-
    tion is resumed with ubi . . . sim (229) and continues through line 234.
229 *bōs, bovis (m), ox, bull.   asellus, -ī (m), ass, donkey.
    coniungō, coniungere (3), coniunxī, coniunctum, to join together.
230 *nequeō, nequīre (irreg.), nequīvī or nequiī, to be unable. pariter, equally.
    *asinus, -ī (m), ass, donkey. lutum, -ī (n), mud, dirt.
231 magis haud: = haud magis.
    nātus . . . sim: perfect subjunctive of nāscor, "I should (never) have been born."
    quasi: = quam sī, "than if."
232 inīquus, -a, -um, uneven, unequal, ill-matched. inīquiōre: "quite ill-matched," "un-
        fair." tē ūtar inīquiōre: "I would find you quite ill-matched."
233 neutrubi, in neither place. stabilis, -is, -e, firm, steady, stable.
    stabulum, -ī (n), standing-place, dwelling.
    dīvertium, -ī (n), parting of ways, turning point, crisis, divorce.
234 mordex, mordicis (m), an incisor tooth.
    scindō, scindere (3), scicidī or scidī, scissum, to split, tear apart, rend.
    incursō (1), to charge at, attack.
235 trānscendō, trānscendere (3), trānscendī, trānscēnsum, to climb across, step over.

204 **MEG.** *(alone and perplexed)* Crēdō edepol, ubi mentiōnem ego fēcerō dē fīliā,
205   mī ut dēspondeat, sē ā mē dērīdērī rēbitur;
206   neque illō quisquam est alter hodiē ex paupertāte parcior.
     EUC. *(returning, obviously much relieved, and muttering to himself)*
207   Dī mē servant, salva rēs est. Salvum est sī quid nōn perit.
208   Nimis male timuī. Priusquam intrō rediī, exanimātus fuī.
     (now giving his attention to Megadorus in a more courteous fashion)
209   Redeō ad tē, Megadōre, sī quid mē vīs. **MEG.** Habeō grātiam.
210   Quaesō, quod tē percontābor, nē id tē pigeat prōloquī.
211 **EUC.** *(aside)* Dum quidem nē quid percontēris quod nōn libeat prōloquī.
212 **MEG.** Dīc mihi, quālī mē arbitrāre genere prōgnātum? **EUC.** Bonō.
213 **MEG.** Quid fidē? **EUC.** Bonā. **MEG.** Quid factīs? **EUC.** Neque malīs
     neque improbīs.
214 **MEG.** Aetātem meam scīs? **EUC.** Sciō esse grandem, item ut pecūniam.
215 **MEG.** Certē edepol equidem tē cīvem sine malā omnī malitiā
216   semper sum arbitrātus et nunc arbitror. **EUC.** *(aside)* Aurum huic olet.
217   *(to Megadorus)* Quid nunc mē vīs? **MEG.** Quoniam tū mē et ego tē
     quālis sīs sciō,
218   quae rēs rēctē vertat mihique tibique tuaeque fīliae,
219   fīliam tuam mī uxōrem poscō. Prōmitte hoc fore.
220 **EUC.** *(peevishly)* Heia, Megadōre, haud decōrum facinus tuīs factīs facis,
221   ut inopem atque innoxium ab tē atque ab tuīs mē irrīdeās.
222   Nam dē tē neque rē neque verbīs meruī ut facerēs quod facis.
223 **MEG.** *(defensively)* Neque edepol ego tē dērīsum veniō neque dērīdeō,
224   neque dignum arbitror. **EUC.** Cūr igitur poscis meam nātam tibi?
225 **MEG.** Ut propter mē tibi sit melius mihique propter tē et tuōs.
226 **EUC.** Venit hoc mihi, Megadōre, in mentem, tē esse hominem dīvitem,
227   factiōsum, mē autem esse hominem pauperum pauperrimum;
228   nunc sī fīliam locāverim meam tibi, in mentem venit
229   tē bovem esse et mē esse asellum: ubi tēcum coniunctus sim,
230   ubi onus nequeam ferre pariter, iaceam ego asinus in lutō,
231   tū mē bōs magis haud respiciās, nātus quasi numquam sim.
232   Et tē ūtar inīquiōre et meus mē ordō irrīdeat,
233   neutrubi habeam stabile stabulum, sī quid dīvertī sit:
234   asinī mē mordicibus scindant, bovēs incursent cornibus.
235   Hoc magnum est perīculum, ab asinīs ad bovēs trānscendere.

1. What does Megadorus feel that Euclio will think when he asks to marry his daughter? (204–205)
2. What did Euclio find inside the house? (207) What were his feelings before he went inside? (208)
3. What four questions does Megadorus ask Euclio about himself? (212–214)
4. To what does Euclio compare Megadorus' age? (214)
5. What conclusion does Euclio draw (216) from Megadorus' flattery in lines 215–216?
6. How does Euclio respond to Megadorus' proposal? (220–222)
7. How does Megadorus justify his marriage proposal, when challenged by Euclio? (225)
8. To what two animals does Euclio compare himself and Megadorus? (229)
9. What does Euclio think would happen to him if he were connected with Megadorus through marriage? (230–235)

236 **Quam . . . proximē . . . tam optimum**: "the nearer . . . the better."
    probus, -a, -um, good, upright, virtuous (a term designating the upper class of society).
    propinquitās, propinquitātis (*f*), nearness, closeness of family relationship, kinship.
    adiungō, adiungere (3), **adiūnxī, adiūnctum**, to connect, associate.
237 ***condiciō, condiciōnis** (*f*), contract, match.
    ***auscultō** (1), to listen to (+ accusative), heed, obey (+ dative).
238 **dēs**: subjunctive in a prohibition.
239 **dum modo**, provided that (+ subjunctive). ***dōtātus, -a, -um**, provided with a dowry.
240 **Eō**: "For this reason," i.e., **nē . . . cēnseās**.
241 **prō Iuppiter**: "by Jupiter!"
242 **dispereō, disperīre** (*irreg.*), **disperiī**, to perish, be destroyed totally.
    ***crepō, crepāre** (1), **crepuī**, to make any kind of loud noise.
243 **hortus, -ī** (*m*), garden.
    cōnfodiō, cōnfodere (3), **cōnfōdī, cōnfossum**, to dig up. Supply **servōs** as subject of the infinitive.
244 **certiōrem facere**, to inform someone.
    fastīdiō, (4), to regard or treat with disdain or distaste, scorn, turn away from (+ genitive).
246 **amīcitia, -ae** (*f*), friendship.
247 ***opulentus, -a, -um**, wealthy, opulent. **petītum**: supine expressing purpose.
248 ***congredior, congredī** (3), **congressus sum**, to approach. **rem gerere**, to carry on.
249 **illaec**: = **illa** (fem. nom. sing.) + **-ce**.
    sērō, late, too late.
250 **ēlinguō** (1), to tear the tongue out. **rādīx, rādīcis** (*f*), root.
251 **cuivīs**: "to whomsoever you wish." **castrō** (1), to emasculate, castrate.
253 **senectus, -a, -um**, old, aged.
    lūdus, -ī (*m*), sport, play. **lūdōs facere aliquem**, to make a fool of someone. **quem . . . faciās**: relative clause of characteristic.
    meritum, -ī (*n*), that which one deserves. **meritō meō**: "as I deserve."
254 **cōpia, -ae** (*f*), (here) possibility, chance.
255 **etiam**: expressing impatience, "now will you . . . ?"
256 **spondeō, spondēre** (2), **spopondī, spōnsum**, to promise in marriage.
257 **Istuc**: = **istud** + **-ce. Istuc dī bene**: supply **vertant** or **faciant**.
    facitō: future imperative.
    ***meminī, meminisse** (**meminī** *is a perfect with present force*), to remember.
      memineris: perfect subjunctive in form with the force of a present subjunctive.
258 **convēnisse**: "that you have agreed." ***afferō, afferre** (*irreg.*), **attulī, allātum**, to bring.
259 **quō . . . pactō**: "how."
    perplexor, perplexārī (1), to muddle up, twist. **perplexārī**: supply **rēs**, "affairs," "matters," as object.
260 **pactum, -ī** (*n*), agreement, that which has been agreed upon.
    pacīscor, pacīscī (3), **pactus sum**, to arrange, to agree to as one's part of a bargain.
      pactum est: "(it) has been agreed." **quod**: = **quoad**, as far as, as long as.
262 **quae**: = **aliquae** (after **num**). **optima**: supply **causa est ut faciāmus**.
263 **numquid**, interrogative word introducing a question where a negative reply is assumed.
    Istuc: "Just that," referring to the arrangement about the dowry.
264 ***heus** (*interjection used to attract a person's attention; pronounced as one syllable*), hey there!
    ***properē**, quickly, without delay. ***macellum, -ī** (*n*), market. **strēnuē**, briskly, quickly.

236	MEG. *(reassuringly)* Quam ad probōs propinquitāte proximē tē adiūnxeris,
237	tam optimum est. Tū condiciōnem hanc accipe, auscultā mihi,
238	atque eam dēspondē mī. EUC. At nihil est dōtis quod dem. MEG. Nē
	dēs.
239	Dum modo mōrāta rēctē veniat, dōtāta est satis.
240	EUC. *(with a forced attempt at humor)* Eō dīcō, nē mē thēsaurōs repperisse cēnseās.
241	MEG. Nōvī, nē doceās. Dēspondē. EUC. Fīat. *(The sound of digging is heard*
	off stage, and Euclio becomes agitated.) Sed prō Iuppiter,
242	num ego disperiī? MEG. Quid tibi est? EUC. *(rushing into his house)*
	Quid crepuit quasi ferrum modo?
243	MEG. *(unaware of Euclio's departure)* Hīc apud mē hortum cōnfodere iussī.
	(discovering Euclio's absence) Sed ubi hic est homō?
244, 245	Abiit neque mē certiōrem fēcit. Fastīdit meī,
246	quod videt mē suam amīcitiam velle: mōre hominum facit;
247	nam sī opulentus it petītum pauperiōris grātiam,
248	pauper metuit congredī, per metum male rem gerit.
249	Īdem, quandō occāsiō illaec periit, post sērō cupit.
	EUC. *(returning and threatening Staphyla in the house)*
250	Sī hercle ego tē nōn ēlinguandam dederō usque ab rādīcibus,
251	imperō auctorque sum ut tū mē cuivīs castrandum locēs.
252	MEG. *(annoyed)* Videō hercle ego tē mē arbitrārī, Euclio, hominem idōneum,
253	quem senectā aetāte lūdōs faciās, haud meritō meō.
254	EUC. Neque edepol, Megadōre, faciō, neque, sī cupiam, cōpia est.
255	MEG. Quid nunc? Etiam mihi dēspondēs fīliam? EUC. Illīs lēgibus,
256	cum illā dōte quam tibi dīxī. MEG. Spondēsne ergō? EUC. Spondeō.
257	MEG. Istuc dī bene— EUC. *(interrupting)* Ita dī faciant. Illud facitō ut memineris,
258	convēnisse ut nē quid dōtis mea ad tē afferret fīlia.
259	MEG. Meminī. EUC. At sciō quō vōs soleātis pactō perplexārī:
260	pactum nōn pactum est, nōn pactum pactum est, quod vōbīs libet.
261	MEG. Nūlla controversia mihi tēcum erit. Sed nūptiās
262	num quae causa est hodiē quīn faciāmus? EUC. Immō edepol optima.
263	MEG. Ībō igitur, parābō. Numquid mē vīs? EUC. Istuc. Ī et valē.
	MEG. *(calling to his steward in the house)*
264	Heus, Strobīle, sequere properē mē ad macellum strēnuē.
	(Strobilus comes out of the house and departs with Megadorus toward
	the forum.)

1. **How does Megadorus try to refute Euclio's argument?** (236–237)
2. **What is Euclio's protest in line 238?**
3. **What does Megadorus mention as compensation for the lack of a dowry?** (239)
4. **Why does Euclio claim he brought the subject up in the first place?** (240)
5. **Does Euclio consent to Megadorus' wish?** (241)
6. **What does Megadorus make of Euclio's hasty departure?** (244–249)
7. **Which man now accuses the other of making fun of him?** (252–253)
8. **What agreement is reached?** (255–256) **What about the dowry?** (255–258)
9. **Does Euclio trust Megadorus?** (259–260)
10. **When does Megadorus want the wedding to take place? Does Euclio consent?** (262)

265 **Illic**: = **ille** + **-ce**, "that fellow."
    quid: exclamatory, "how!"
266 **inaudiō** (4), to hear.
267 **eā . . . grātiā**: "for the sake of that" (i.e., the gold).
    affīnitās, affīnitātis (*f*), relationship by marriage.
    obstinō (1), to set one's mind on, determine on.
268 **dēblaterō** (1), to babble.
270 *****ecquid** (*introducing a question*), surely.
    vasculum, -ī (*n*), a small vessel, utensil. **pūrē**, in a clean manner, so as to be clean
    properō (1), (here) to get ready with haste. **ēluō, ēluere** (3), **ēluī, ēlūtum**, to wash
    clean.
272 *****ēcastor**: a woman's oath, like **mecastor** (see note to line 67).
    *****nōn potest**: "it is not possible"; supply **fierī**. **subitus, -a, -um**, sudden, unexpected.
273 **Cūrāta fac sint**: = **Fac ut omnia cūrāta sint.**
275 **exitium, -ī** (*n*), destruction, disaster, ruin.
277 *****occultō** (1), to hide, keep hidden, conceal. **adhūc**, up to the present time.
279 *****malum, -ī** (*n*), trouble, evil. **maeror, maerōris** (*n*), grief.
    mixtus, -a, -um, mixed, mixed with (+ *abl.*). *****bibō, bibere** (3), **bibī**, to drink.
280 *****obsōnō** (1), to purchase or get provisions, do the shopping.
    *****condūcō, condūcere** (3), **condūxī, conductum**, to bring together, hire.
    *****coquus, -ī** (*m*), cook.
281 *****tībīcina, -ae** (*f*), flute player, flute girl. **hāsce**: = **hās** + **-ce**.
    *****forum, -ī** (*n*), public square in the center of a town, marketplace.
    ēdīcō, ēdīcere (3), **ēdīxī, ēdictum**, to state, declare.
282 *****dispertiō, dispertīre** (4), **dispertīvī, dispertītum**, to divide up.
    *****obsōnium, -ī** (*n*), provisions (of all sorts) for a meal. The word is taken by Anthrax
    in the next line to include the cooks.
    bifāriam (*adv.*), in two ways.
283 **prōpalam** (*adv.*), very openly.
284 **quō**: = **aliquō** (after **sī**), to some place, somewhere.
285 **bellus, -a, -um**, pretty, fine, excellent (often ironical).
    pudīcus, -a, -um, chaste, pure. **prostibulum, -ī** (*n*), prostitute. Vocative here.
286 **post** (*adv.*), in the rear, behind. Part of an obscene joke here; supply **tē dīvidere** with
    vellet (subjunctive in a present contrary-to-fact condition).
    haud nōn vellēs: "you would (certainly) wish."
287 **aliōversum**, in a different manner or sense.
    dīxeram: pluperfect for perfect.
288 **īnsimulō** (1), to bring forward as a charge, allege.
291 **adeō**: emphasizing **eī**. *****dīmidium, -ī** (*n*), half.
292 **itidem**, in the same way, just so.
293 *****nempe**, without doubt, of course, to be sure.

265 EUC. *(alone)* Illic hinc abiit. Dī immortālēs, obsecrō, aurum quid valet!
266   Crēdō ego illum iam inaudīvisse mī esse thēsaurum domī.
267   Id inhiat, eā affinitātem hanc obstināvit grātiā.
     (calling Staphyla out of his house)
268   Ubi tū es quae dēblaterāvistī iam vīcīnīs omnibus
269   meae mē fīliae datūrum dōtem? Heus, Staphyla, tē vocō.
270   Ecquid audīs? *(Staphyla hurries out of the house.)* Vascula intus pūrē
     properā atque ēlue:
271   fīliam dēspondī ego: hodiē huic nūptum Megadōrō dabō.
272 STA. *(anxiously)* Dī bene vertant. Vērum ēcastor nōn potest, subitum est nimis.
273 EUC. Tacē atque abī. Cūrāta fac sint cum ā forō redeam domum;
274   atque aedīs occlūde; iam ego hīc aderō. *(Euclio departs to the right to-*
     ward the forum.) STA. *(alone and worried)* Quid ego nunc agam?
275   Nunc nōbis prope adest exitium, mihi atque erīlī fīliae;
276   nunc probrum atque partitūdō prope adest ut fīat palam;
277   quod cēlātum atque occultātum est usque adhūc, nunc nōn potest.
278   Ībō intrō, ut erus quae imperāvit facta, cum veniat, sint.
279   Nam ēcastor malum maerōre metuō nē mixtum bibam. *(Staphyla sadly*
     enters the house.)

The stage is empty for a few moments. Suddenly Strobilus (STR.) returns
from the forum with two cooks, Anthrax (AN.) and Congrio (CON.), and
their assistants and with two flute girls, Phrygia and Eleusium. These are
followed by two live sheep and various attendants carrying provisions
and cooking utensils.

280 STR. *(imperiously)* Postquam obsōnāvit erus et condūxit coquōs   DIALOGUE
281   tibicīnāsque hāsce apud forum, ēdīxit mihi
282   ut dispertīrem obsōnium hīc bifāriam.
283 AN. Mē quidem hercle, dīcam prōpalam, nōn dīvidēs;
284   sī quō tū tōtum mē īre vīs, operam dabō.
285 CON. *(to Anthrax)* Bellum et pudīcum vērō prostibulum populī,
286   post sī quis vellet, tē haud nōn vellēs dīvidī.
287 STR. *(to Anthrax)* Atque ego istuc, Anthrax, aliōversum dīxeram,
288   nōn istuc quod tū īnsimulās. Sed erus nūptiās
289   meus hodiē faciet. AN. Cuius dūcit fīliam?
290 STR. Vīcīnī huius Eucliōnis hinc ē proxumō.
291   Eī adeō obsōnī hinc iussit dīmidium darī,
292   coquum alterum itidemque alteram tibīcinam.
293 AN. Nempe hūc dīmidium dīcis, dīmidium domum?
294 STR. Nempe sīcut dīcis.

1. **What does Euclio think is Megadorus' reason for wanting to marry Phaedria?**
   (265–267)
2. **What is Staphyla's initial reaction to the news of the betrothal?** (272) **What is**
   her subsequent response? (274–279)
3. **What has Strobilus been instructed to do with what has been procured?**
   (280–282)
4. **What objection does Anthrax raise? How does Congrio turn it into a joke?**
   (283–286)
5. **How are things to be divided up?** (291–294)

295 **obsōnor, obsōnārī** (1), **obsōnātus sum**: = **obsōnō** (see 280).
296 ***vah** (*interjection expressing astonishment*), ah! oh!   **Quid negōtī est**: partitive genitive, "What's the problem?" "What's the trouble?"
297 **pūmex, pūmicis** (*m*), pumice, volcanic rock.
   aridus, -a, -um, dry, withered, miserly.   **atque**, (here) as.
298 ***tandem**, finally, now.   **Ita esse** . . .: exclamatory infinitive, "It's just as you say!" One or more lines have been lost from the text. Strobilus begins to tell stories about Euclio's miserliness. The lost line or lines may have said, "When he loses something even trifling, he thinks (**exīstimat**). . . . ," leading into the indirect statement in line 299.
299 **ērādīcō** (1), to tear up by the roots, destroy utterly.
300 ***quīn**, (here) indeed, in fact, even.   **fidem**: i.e., Euclio calls upon gods and men as witnesses.
301 **tigillum, -ī** (*n*), a small piece of wood (**tignum, -ī**, *n*). **dē suō tigillō**: i.e., if even a small piece of wood is burned on his hearth.   **fūmus, -ī** (*m*), smoke.
   sī quā: = **sī aliquā. aliquā** (*adv.*), in some way or other, somehow.
302 **dormītum**: supine expressing purpose.   **follis, follis** (*m*), bag, sack.
   obstringō, obstringere (3), **obstrīnxī, obstrictum**, to tie firmly.
   *ob (+ acc.), on account of, in front of.   ***gula, -ae** (*f*), throat, gullet, (here) mouth.
303 ***anima, -ae** (*f*), breath.
304 **obtūrō** (1), to block, stop up.
   guttur, gutturis (*m; n* in later Latin), throat.
307 **quōmodo**: i.e., "how he acts."
308 ***plōrō** (1), to lament, grieve, be distressed (to do something) (+ infinitive).
   *lavō (1), to wash, bathe.   **profundō, profundere** (3), **profūdī, profūsum**, to pour out.
309 **talentum, -ī** (*n*), the Athenian talent (a very large sum of money).
   exōrō (1), to obtain by asking.   ***potis** or **pote**, possible. **pote** (**esse**), to be possible.
310 **quī**: see note to line 187.
311 **ūtendam** . . . **rogēs**: "you should ask to borrow."
312 **ipsī**: dative of reference.
   *prīdem, formerly, once.   **tōnsor, tōnsōris** (*m*), barber, nail-cutter.   **unguīs**: = **unguēs**.
313 **praesegmen, praesegminis** (*n*), clipping.
314 ***mortālis, mortālis** (*m*), human being.   **parcē parcum**: "stingily stingy," "extremely stingy."
316 **pulmentum, -ī** (*n*), small portion of meat or fish eaten as a starter to a meal.
   ēripiō, ēripere (3), **ēripuī, ēreptum**, to seize, snatch away. **eī**: dative of reference or separation.
   *milvus, -ī (*m*), bird of prey, kite.
317 ***praetor, praetōris** (*m*), praetor (a magistrate at Rome concerned chiefly with judicial functions).
   dēplōrābundus, -a, -um, complaining bitterly.
318 **īnfit**, (he) begins (+ infinitive).   ***ēiulō** (1), to shriek, wail.
319 **vador, vadārī** (1), **vadātus sum**, to bind over by bail to appear in court.
320 **sēscentī, -ae, -a**, six hundred (proverbially an infinitely large number).
   *memorō (1), to mention, speak of, tell.   **ōtium, -ī** (*n*), leisure.
321 **vestrum**: genitive of **vōs**.
322 **ut**, as.
323 **Coquum ergō dīcō**: "Well, I mean a cook."
324 **nūndinālis, -is, -e**, of or belonging to market days. Here of a cook fit to be employed only on market days, when more cooks were needed. From **nūndinae, -ārum** (*f pl*), market day (occurring at regular intervals of eight days, i.e., every ninth day by Roman reckoning). **in nōnum diem**: "for market day."
325 ***coquō, coquere** (3), **coxī, coctum**, to cook. ***coctum**: supine expressing purpose.
326 **vituperō** (1), to blame, disparage.
   trifurcifer, trifurciferī (*m*), triple rogue. From **furcifer, furciferī** (*m*), one who is punished with a "fork," a scoundrel, villain. From **furca, -ae** (*f*), fork, a forked frame put on a man's neck as punishment, his arms being fastened to the projecting ends.

294		AN. Quid? Hīc nōn poterat dē suō
295		senex obsōnārī fīliae nūptiīs?
296	STR.	Vah! AN. Quid negōtī est? STR. Quid negōtī sit rogās?
297		Pūmex nōn aequē est aridus atque hīc est senex.
298	AN.	Aisne tandem? CON. Ita esse ut dīcis! STR. . . . exīstimat
299		suam rem perīisse sēque ērādīcārī.
300		Quīn dīvōrum atque hominum clāmat continuō fidem,
301		dē suō tigillō fūmus sī quā exit forās.
302		Quīn, cum it dormītum, follem obstringit ob gulam.
303	AN.	Cūr? STR. Nē quid animae forte āmittat dormiēns.
304	AN.	Etiamne obtūrat īnferiōrem gutturem,
305		nē quid animae forte āmittat dormiēns?
306	STR.	Haec mihi tē ut tibi mē aequum est, crēdō, crēdere.
307	AN.	Immō equidem crēdō. STR. At scīsne etiam quōmodo?
308		Aquam hercle plōrat, cum lavat, profundere.
309	AN.	Cēnsēsne talentum magnum exōrārī pote
310		ab istōc sene, ut det quī fīāmus līberī?
311	STR.	Famem hercle ūtendam sī rogēs, numquam dabit.
312		Quīn ipsī prīdem tōnsor unguīs dēmpserat:
313		collēgit, omnia abstulit praesegmina.
314	AN.	Edepol mortālem parcē parcum praedicās.
315	STR.	Cēnsēsne vērō adeō esse parcum et miserē vīvere?
316		Pulmentum prīdem ēripuit eī milvus:
317		homō ad praetōrem dēplōrābundus venit;
318		īnfit ibi postulāre plōrāns, ēiulāns,
319		ut sibi licēret milvum vadārī.
320		sēscenta sunt quae memorem, sī sit ōtium.

(changing the subject and addressing the two cooks, Anthrax and Congrio)

321		Sed uter vestrum est celerior? Memorā mihi.
322	AN.	Ego, ut multō melior. STR. Coquum ego, nōn fūrem rogō.
323	AN.	Coquum ergō dīcō. STR. *(to Congrio)* Quid tū āis? CON. *(posing)* Sīc sum ut vidēs.
	AN.	*(giving an insulting description of Congrio)*
324		Coquus ille nūndinālis est, in nōnum diem
325		solet īre coctum. CON. *(responding with anger)* Tūne, trium litterārum homō,
326		mē vituperās? Fūr! AN. *(throwing the insult back at Congrio)* Etiam fūr, trifurcifer!

1. **What does Anthrax wonder about?** (294–295)
2. **What is implied by the simile in line 297?**
3. **What five examples of Euclio's stinginess does Strobilus give?** (300–301, 302–303, 308, 312–313, and 316–319)
4. **How does Anthrax react to each example of Euclio's stinginess?** (303, 304–305, 307, 309–310, and 314)
5. **How does Strobilus change the subject in line 321?**
6. **What do Anthrax and Congrio end up calling each other?** (325–326)

29

327 **agnus, -ī** (*m*), lamb. **pinguis, -is, -e**, fat.
328 **licet**, very well, all right, okay.
329 **illō**, to that place.
330 **iniūriā** (*abl. sing. as adv.*), unjustly.
333 **sānē**, soundly, certainly, truly (here merely adds to the force of the imperative and
     need not be translated).
   Phrygia, -ae (*f*) (*Greek word*), name of a slave girl from Phrygia. The name is appro-
     priate for a flute girl, since a particular kind of flute was called **tibiae Phrygiae**.
   Eleusium, -ī (*n*), the name of the other flute girl, derived from Eleusis, the site of
     the mysteries of Demeter (Persephone) in Attica, west of Athens.
334 **subdolus, -a, -um**, cunning, sly, deceitful.
335 **hūcine**: = **hūc** + **-ne** (a particle added for emphasis).
   dētrūdō, dētrūdere (3), **dētrūsī, dētrūsum**, to push away, drive.
336 **ravis, ravis** (*f*), hoarseness.
337 **dētur**: why subjunctive?
338 **quod faciās perit**: "whatever you do goes for nothing."
339 **quī** (*adverbial abl.*), how? how so? **prīncipiō**, first of all, to start with.
340 **turba, -ae** (*f*), disorder, crowd. **istīc**, there, over there. **sī quid**: = **sī aliquid**. **ūtī**:
     from **ūtor**, here with accusative.
341 **affertō**: future imperative.
   perdō, perdere (3), **perdidī, perditum**, to ruin, lose, waste. **operam perdere**, to waste
     one's effort in doing something (here with the infinitive **poscere** instead of usual
     gerund in the ablative).
343 **supellex, supellicis** (*f*), household utensils, stuff, furniture.
   argenteus, -a, -um, of silver.
344 **quispiam, quaepiam, quippiam** (**quidpiam**), someone, anybody, something, anything.
345 **facile**, easily.
   abstineō, abstinēre (2), **abstinuī, abstentum**, to keep away, restrain oneself, abstain.
     quod (344) . . . **abstinēre**: "to abstain from which."
   obviam (*adv.*), in the way, available.
346 **comprehendō, comprehendere** (3), **comprehendī, comprehēnsum**, to seize, arrest.
347 **vinciō, vincīre** (3), **vīnxī, vīnctum**, to bind, tie up.
   puteus, -ī (*m*), well, pit for storing grain or confining prisoners.
348 **quippe quī**, inasmuch as.
349 **quid**: the interrogative pronoun is retained where one would expect the relative.
   hāc, this way.

The slap-stick humor of the scene with the cooks may owe something to earlier traditions of farce as seen on this fourth century B.C. vase painting of thieves pulling a miser off his money chest.

327   **STR.** *(restraining Anthrax)* Tacē nunciam tū, atque agnum hinc uter est pinguior
328   cape atque abī intrō ad nōs. **AN.** *(choosing a sheep and leading it into*
           Megadorus' house) Licet. **STR.** *(giving the other sheep to Congrio)*
           Tū, Congriō,
329   hunc sūme atque abī intrō illō *(pointing to Euclio's house)*, et vōs
           (pointing to some of the assistants) illum *(pointing to Congrio)*
           sequiminī.
330   Vōs cēterī *(pointing to the remaining assistants)* īte hūc ad nōs *(pointing*
           to Megadorus' house).

Some of the group of assistants follow Anthrax into Megadorus' house,
and the rest gather around Congrio to follow him into Euclio's house.

330   **CON.** *(indignant)* Hercle iniūriā
331   dispertīvistī: pinguiōrem agnum istī habent.
332   **STR.** At nunc tibi dabitur pinguior tībīcina.
333   *(to Phrygia)* Ī sānē cum illō *(pointing to Congrio)*, Phrygia. *(to*
           Eleusium) Tū autem, Eleusium,
334   hūc intrō abī ad nōs *(pointing to Megadorus' house, which Eleusium*
           enters). **CON.** Ō Strobīle subdole,
335   hūcine *(pointing to Euclio's house)* dētrūsistī mē ad senem parcissimum?
336   ubi sī quid poscam, usque ad ravim poscam prius
337   quam quicquam dētur. **STR.** Stultus es, et sine grātiā est
338   ibi rēctē facere, quandō quod faciās perit.
339   **CON.** Quī vērō? **STR.** Rogitās? Iam prīncipiō in aedibus
340   turba istīc *(pointing to Euclio's house)* nūlla tibi erit: sī quid ūtī volēs,
341   domō ab tē affertō, nē operam perdās poscere.
342   Hīc autem apud nōs magna turba ac familia est,
343   supellex, aurum, vestis, vāsa argentea:
344   ibi sī perierit quippiam (quod tē sciō
345   facile abstinēre posse, sī nihil obviam est),
346   dīcant: coquī abstulērunt, comprehendite,
347   vincīte, verberāte, in puteum condite.
348   Hōrum tibi istīc nihil ēveniet (quippe quī
349   ubi quid surripiās nihil est). Sequere hāc *(pointing to Euclio's house)*
           mē. **CON.** *(obeying)* Sequor.

1. **How does Strobilus settle the argument between Anthrax and Congrio?** (327–328)
2. **Why does Congrio think the division has been unfair?** (330–331)
3. **How does Strobilus try to even things up?** (332)
4. **What does Congrio complain about next?** (335) **What particular problem does he think he will encounter in Euclio's house?** (336–337)
5. **What does Strobilus mean when he suggests that his good intentions have been wasted?** (337–338)
6. **Why, according to Strobilus, is it better to work in Euclio's house?** (339–341)
7. **What danger is there in working in Megadorus' house?** (342–347)
8. **What will happen to the cooks if anything is missing from the house where they are working?** (344–347)

350 **prōdeō, prōdīre** (*irreg.*), **prōdiī, prōditum**, to come forward, come out.
ōstium, -ī (*n*), door.
353 **mittere**: the passive infinitive, **mittī**, would be expected here; or supply **mē** as the subject of **mittere**.
355 **quī** (*adverbial abl.*), how? how so?
tēmētum, -ī (*n*), wine. Wine was not permitted at the festivals called **Cereris nūptiae**.
356 *****ipse**: here = **dominus**, the master himself, the master of the house.
357 *****lignum, -ī** (*n*), firewood.
asser, asseris (*m*), a wooden beam, rafter.
358 *****forīs** (*adv.*), outside.
359 **impūrātus, -a, -um**, filthy, polluted (usually as a term of abuse).
Volcānus, -ī (*m*), Vulcan, the god of fire (by *metonymy*, the use of one word to suggest some other, related idea) fire.
360***** **mercēs, mercēdis** (*f*), wages, pay.
361 **combūrō, combūrere** (3), **combussī, combustum**, to burn up.
364 **servem**: "look after."
365 **Nisi ūnum hoc faciam, ut. . . .** : i.e., there would be trouble, "unless I see to this one thing, that. . . . "
366 **sūrsum**, from below, upward, up.
subdūcō, subdūcere (3), **subdūxī, subductum**, to draw from under or below, lift up.
corbula, -ae (*f*), a small basket.
367 *****deorsum** (*pronounced as two syllables*), down, down below
comedō, comēsse (*irreg.*), **comēdī, comēsum**, to eat.
368 **superus, -a, -um**, that which is above, upper, higher. **superī, -ōrum** (*m pl*), they who are above, the inhabitants of the upper world, the gods above.
incēnātus, -a, -um, without dinner. **cēnātus, -a, -um**, having dined or eaten.
īnferus, -a, -um, situated below, lower, down below. **īnferī, -ōrum** (*m pl*), the inhabitants of the underworld (both the dead and the infernal deities).
369 **verba**: i.e., mere words (rather than deeds).
370 **rapācida, -ae** (*f*), robber. A comic patronymic formed from the adjective **rapāx, rapācis**, rapacious, given to stealing things.

Strobilus' presentation of Congrio, his helpers, and Phygria to Staphyla at the door of Euclio's house might have resembled this scene from a play of Plautus' follower, Terence, as illustrated in an early Medieval manuscript.

Strobilus, Congrio, the assistants, Phrygia, and the sheep go toward Eu-
clio's house. Strobilus knocks on the door and calls for Staphyla.

350 **STR.** Heus, Staphyla, prōdī atque ōstium aperī. **STA.** *(from inside)* Quis vocat?
351 **STR.** Strobīlus. **STA.** *(coming out)* Quid vīs? **STR.** Hōs ut accipiās coquōs
352   tībīcinamque obsōniumque in nūptiās.
353   Megadōrus iussit Eucliōnī haec mittere.
    STA. *(disappointed as she looks over the provisions)*
354   Cererīne, Strobīle, hās sunt factūrī nūptiās?
355 **STR.** Quī? **STA.** Quia tēmētī nihil allātum intellegō.
356 **STR.** At iam afferētur, sī ā forō ipse redierit.
357 **STA.** Ligna hīc apud nōs nūlla sunt. **CON.** Sunt asserēs?
358 **STA.** Sunt pol. **CON.** Sunt igitur ligna, nē quaerās forīs.
359 **STA.** Quid, impūrāte? Quamquam Volcānō studēs,
360   cēnaene causā aut tuae mercēdis grātiā
361   nōs nostrās aedīs postulās combūrere?
362 **CON.** Haud postulō. **STR.** *(to Staphyla)* Dūc istōs *(pointing to Congrio, the*
     assistants, and Phrygia) intrō. **STA.** *(bringing up the rear as all but*
     Strobilus enter Euclio's house) Sequiminī.
    STR. *(to the group as they enter Euclio's house)*
363   Cūrāte. *(to himself as he goes toward Megadorus' house)* Ego inter-
     vīsam quid faciant coquī;
364   quōs pol ut ego hodiē servem cūra maxima est.
365   Nisi ūnum hoc faciam, ut in puteō cēnam coquant:
366   inde coctam sūrsum subdūcēmus corbulīs.
367   Sī autem deorsum comedent sī quid coxerint,
368   superī incēnātī sunt et cēnātī īnferī.
369   Sed verba hīc faciō, quasi negōtī nīl sit,
370   rapācidārum ubi tantum sit in aedibus.
     (Exit into Megadorus' house.)

1. **What is Staphyla disappointed not to find among the provisions?** (354–355)
2. **Of what else does Staphyla note the absence?** (357)
3. **How does Strobilus propose to solve this problem?** (357–358)
4. **How does Staphyla react to Strobilus' proposal?** (359–361)
5. **What is Strobilus' main concern to be?** (363–364)
6. **What idea does Strobilus conceive for keeping the cooks out of trouble?** (365–366)
7. **What possible drawback does that idea have?** (367–368)
8. **What is Strobilus afraid the cooks are doing in Megadorus' house?** (370)

371 **cōnfirmō** (1), to strengthen. **animum . . . cōnfirmāre**: "to strengthen my mind," "to encourage myself."
372 **bene habērem mē**: "I would be happy," "I would enjoy myself."
373 ***piscis, piscis** (*m*), fish. **piscīs**: = **piscēs**.
374 ***cārus, -a, -um**, dear, expensive. **agnīna, -ae** (*f*), lamb's flesh. **būbula, -ae** (*f*), beef.
375 **vitulīna, -ae** (*f*), calf's flesh, veal.
cētus, -ī (*m*), the flesh of a large sea-animal such as whale, porpoise, or dolphin.
porcīna, -ae (*f*), pork meat.
376 **eō**: "for this reason," (**quod**) **aes nōn erat**.
377 **illinc**, from there.
quī (*adverbial abl.*), by which means, whereby, wherewith.
378 **impūrus, -a, -um**, dirty, abominable, foul. **illīs impūrīs omnibus**: Euclio is referring to the tradesmen in the marketplace.
manum adīre (+ *dat.*), to cheat, deceive. Euclio thinks he has cheated the tradesmen by not buying anything from them.
379 **interviās** (*adv.*), on the way (home).
380 ***occipiō, occipere** (3), **occēpī, occeptum**, to take up, begin.
fēstus diēs, a holiday, feast day.
prōdigō, prōdigere (3), **prōdēgī**, to drive forth, waste, squander.
381 **profēstus, -a, -um**, a nonholiday, ordinary working day.
egeō, egēre (2), **eguī**, to need, find oneself in need, lack (the necessities of life, especially money).
peperceris (from **parcō**): i.e., live sparingly.
382 **venter, ventris** (*m*), belly. ***cor, cordis** (*n*), heart, mind.
ēdō, ēdere (3), **ēdidī, ēditum**, to give forth, declare.
383 **accessit**: here used in a political sense, "sided with," "cast its vote for." **sententiam**: another political term, "opinion," "motion." Translate, "my mind voted for the motion to. . . ." "I made up my mind to. . . ."
384 **quam** (+ *superlative*), as . . . as possible. **minimus, -a, -um**, smallest, least.
385 **tūsculum, -ī** (*n*), a little frankincense (**tūs, tūris**, *n*).
hāsce: = **hās** + **-ce. flōreus, -a, -um**, made or consisting of flowers.
386 **haec**: = **hae** (fem. nom. pl.) + **-ce. impōnō, impōnere** (3), **imposuī, impositum**, to place on.
389 **strepitus, -ūs** (*m*), noise. **Numnam**: = an emphatic **num**.
compīlō (1), to rob, pillage.
390 ***aula, -ae** (*f*), pot or jar for cooking.
pote: supply **est**, "if it is possible."
vīcīnia, -ae (*f*), neighborhood, neighbors.
393 **nīmīrum**, without doubt, evidently.
394 **Apollō, Apollinis** (*m*), god of prophecy, music, and archery (protector against thieves; worshiped at Delphi).
***subveniō, subvenīre** (4), **subvēnī, subventum** (+ *dat.*), to come to one's assistance, help.
adiuvō (1), to help.
395 **cōnfīgō, cōnfīgere** (3), **cōnfīxī, cōnfīxum**, to fasten together, pierce.
thēsaurarius, -a, -um, of treasure. Euclio's invocation of Apollo to help against **fūrēs thēsaurāriōs** may allude to an attack on Delphi and its treasuries by the Gauls in 279 B.C.
396 **tālis, -is, -e**, such. **antehāc**, before.
397 ***cessō** (1), to hold back from, hesitate (+ infinitive). **cessō . . . currere**: probably intended here as a question without the usual interrogative particle.
prōrsus, thoroughly, altogether.

34

The stage is empty for a few moments. Then Euclio returns from the forum carrying a package and a few flowers, talking aloud to himself.

371	EUC.	Voluī animum tandem cōnfirmāre hodiē meum,
372		ut bene habērem mē filiae nūptiīs.
373		Veniō ad macellum, rogitō piscīs: indicant
374		cārōs; agnīnam cāram, cāram būbulam,
375		vitulīnam, cētum, porcīnam: cāra omnia.
376		Atque eō fuērunt cāriōra, aes nōn erat.
377		Abeō īrātus illinc, quoniam nihil est quī emam.
378		Ita illīs impūrīs omnibus adiī manum.
379		Deinde ego mēcum cōgitāre interviās
380		occēpī: fēstō diē sī quid prōdēgeris,
381		profēstō egēre liceat, nisi peperceris.
382		Postquam hanc ratiōnem ventrī cordīque ēdidī,
383		accessit animus ad meam sententiam,
384		quam minimō sūmptū fīliam ut nūptum darem.
385		Nunc tūsculum ēmī et hāsce corōnās flōreās:
386		haec impōnentur in focō nostrō Larī,
387		ut fortunātās faciat nātae nūptiās.

(As Euclio reaches center stage near his house, he looks at the open door in consternation and is startled at the noise he hears inside.)

388		Sed quid ego apertās aedīs nostrās cōnspicor?
389		Et strepitus est intus. Numnam ego compīlor miser?
	CON.	*(from inside the house, addressing one of his assistants)*
390		Aulam maiōrem, sī pote, ex vīciniā
391		pete: haec est parva, capere nōn quit. EUC. Ei mihi,
392		periī hercle. Aurum rapitur, aula quaeritur.
393		Nīmīrum occīdor, nisi ego intrō hūc properē properō currere.

(approaching the altar of Apollo and praying)

394		Apollō, quaesō, subvenī mī atque adiuvā,
395		cōnfīge sagittīs fūrēs thēsaurāriōs,
396		quī in rē tālī iam subvēnistī antehāc.
397		*(to himself)* Sed cessō priusquam prōrsus periī currere?

1. **With what has Euclio been concerned?** (371–372)
2. **What did he try to buy at market?** (373–375) **Why didn't he buy?** (375–376)
3. **What were Euclio's feelings and how does he regard the merchants?** (377–378)
4. **How did Euclio rationalize his decision not to buy any food for his daughter's wedding?** (379–381)
5. **To what did Euclio's thoughts then turn?** (383–384)
6. **What did he buy?** (385) **Why?** (386–387)
7. **How is Euclio's house different (388) from the way he ordered it to be when he left for the forum in line 274?**
8. **What does Congrio call for?** (390–391) **What does Euclio think he is doing?** (392)
9. **What does Euclio pray that Apollo do?** (395)

398 **Dromō, Dromōnis** (*m*), a Greek name meaning "Runner."
  dēsquāmō (1), to remove scales (**squāma, -ae,** *f*) from.
  Machaeriō, Machaeriōnis (*m*), a Greek name meaning "Knife," "Cleaver."
399 **conger, congrī** (*m*), eel. **mūrēna, -ae** (*f*), eel, moray. **exdorsuō** (1), to remove the
  backbone from.
  quantum potest, as quickly as possible.
400 **artopta, -ae** (*f*) (*Greek loan word*), bread pan. **ūtendam petō**: "I (will) try to borrow."
401 ***gallus, -ī** (*m*), farmyard cock.
  sapiō, sapere (3), **sapīvī** or **sapiī**, to have taste or good sense, be wise.
402 **glaber, glabra, glabrum**, hairless, smooth, without feathers. **vulsus, -a, -um**, plucked.
  lūdius, -ī (*m*), stage performer, dancer (here of young men with the down plucked
  from their chins).
404 **faciunt officium suum**: ironic = **faciunt clāmōrem**.
405 **itidem**, in the same way, just so, likewise.
406 **attatae**, interjection expressing sudden surprise. **populāris, populāris** (*m*), fellow
  citizen. **incola, -ae** (*f*), inhabitant. **accola, -ae** (*f*), neighbor. **advena, -ae** (*f*), for-
  eigner.
407 **platea, -ae** (*f*) (*Greek loan word*), street. **pateant**: subjunctive in what kind of
  clause?
408 **Baccha, -ae** (*f*) (*Greek loan word*), a female votary of Bacchus, a Bacchante.
  ***bacchānāl, bacchānālis** (*n*), a shrine or site where the rites of Bacchus were cele-
  brated. Here metaphorically of Euclio's house. The celebration of these Greek rites
  had become so obnoxious to Roman authorities that in 186 B.C. the Senate forbade
  them to be celebrated with more than five people present.
  coquinō (1), to cook. **coquinātum**: supine expressing purpose.
409 **discipulus, -ī** (*m*), pupil, trainee (in a trade).
  contundō, contundere (3), **contudī, contūsum**, to pound to pieces, crush, bruise.
410 ***oppidō** (*adv.*), utterly, totally.
  gymnasium, -ī (*n*) (*Greek loan word*), place in which athletic activities were prac-
  ticed. **mē . . . habuit . . . gymnasium**: "he used me as a punching bag."
411 ***attat**: shortened form of **attatae** (406, above).
412 **Sciō quam rem geram**: i.e., flee, as Euclio himself (**ipse magister**, 412a) has taught
  him to do.
413 **ligna . . . praebērī**: Congrio is referring to his having been generously "supplied"
  (beaten) with "wood" (clubs) by Euclio.
  usquam, anywhere. **usquam gentium**: "anywhere in the world." **pulchrē**, in fine
  style, fully, well.
414 **exigō, exigere** (3), **exēgī, exāctum**, to drive out. ***onustus, -a, -um** (+ *gen.* or *abl.*),
  burdened, loaded (with).
415 ***Tenē, tenē!** Stop him! Stop him! **stolidus, -a, -um**, slow, dull, stupid.
416 **trēsvirī, -ōrum** (*m pl*), three men holding an office together, (here) officials empow-
  ered to make arrests and oversee prisons.
  dēferō, dēferre (*irreg.*), **dētulī, dēlātum**, to carry, bring, take information about, report. **nōmen dēferre**, to report a person to the authorities.
417 **comminor, comminārī** (1), **comminātus sum** (+ *dat.*), to threaten.
418 **factum**: supply **esse**. **fodiō, fodere** (3), **fōdī, fossum**, to dig, pierce, stab.
419 **vīvat**: = (simply) sit.
420 **industria, -ae** (*f*), industry, purposefulness. **dē industriā**: "deliberately."
  ***plūs** (*adv.*), more. Modifies **male . . . faciam. male plūs . . . faciam** (+ *dat.*): "I
  would ill-treat more."
  ***libēns, libentis**, willingly, gladly. Modified by **amplius**, "more."
422 **mollis, -is, -e**, soft. **magis**: reinforcing the comparative **mollior**.
  cinaedus, -ī (*m*) (*Greek loan word*), effeminate man, boy kept by a homosexual,
  (here) dancer or actor in a pantomime.
423 ***tactiō, tactiōnis** (*f*), a touching, touch. Used in Plautus as a verbal noun followed
  by an accusative object; **quid tibi nōs tactiō est?** = **cūr nōs tetigistī?**
  mendīcus, -a, -um, beggarly, mean.
424 **minus** (*adv.*), less.

Euclio rushes into his house thoroughly alarmed; at the same moment Anthrax comes out of Megadorus' house, giving orders to his assistants within.

398	**AN.**	Dromō, dēsquāmā piscīs. Tū, Machaeriō,
399		congrum, mūrēnam exdorsuā quantum potest.
400		Ego hinc artoptam ex proximō ūtendam petō
401		ā Congriōne. Tū istum gallum, sī sapis,
402		glabriōrem reddēs mihi quam vulsus lūdius est.

(Sounds of commotion are heard in Euclio's house.)

403	Sed quid hoc clāmōris oritur hinc ex proximō?
404	Coquī hercle, crēdō, faciunt officium suum.
405	Fugiam intrō, nē quid hīc itidem turbae sit.

Anthrax returns into Megadorus' house; at the same moment Congrio, carving knife in hand, and his assistants burst out of Euclio's house, where they have been beaten by the miser. Congrio calls upon imaginary people in the road to clear a way for his flight.

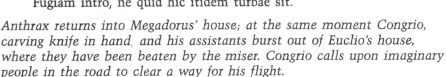

406	**CON.**	Attatae! Cīvēs, populārēs, incolae, accolae, advenae omnēs,	SONG
407		date viam quā fugere liceat, facite tōtae plateae pateant.	
408		Neque ego umquam nisi hodiē ad Bacchās vēnī in bacchānāl coquinātum,	
409		ita mē miserum et meōs discipulōs fūstibus male contudērunt.	
410		Tōtus doleō atque oppidō periī, ita mē iste habuit senex gymnasium;	
411		attat, periī hercle ego miser.	

(Euclio appears at the doorway in pursuit, armed with a cudgel.)

411a	Aperit bacchānāl, adest,
412	sequitur. *(about to flee)* Sciō quam rem geram: hoc
412a	ipse magister mē docuit.
413	Neque ligna ego usquam gentium praebērī vīdī pulchrius,
414	itaque omnīs exēgit forās, mē atque hōs, onustōs fūstibus.

415	**EUC.**	Redī. Quō fugis nunc? Tenē, tenē! **CON.** *(stopping)* Quid, stolide, clāmās?
416	**EUC.**	Quia ad trēsvirōs iam ego dēferam nōmen tuum. **CON.** Quam ob rem?
417	**EUC.**	Quia cultrum habēs. **CON.** Coquum decet. **EUC.** Quid comminātus es
418		mihi? **CON.** Istuc male factum arbitror, quia nōn latus fōdī.
419	**EUC.**	Homō nūllus est tē scelestior quī vīvat hodiē,
420		neque cui ego dē industriā amplius male plūs libēns faciam.

CON. *(rubbing his head and shoulders)*

421	Pol etsī taceās, palam id quidem est: rēs ipsa testis est;
422	ita fūstibus sum mollior magis quam ūllus cinaedus.
423	Sed quid tibi nōs tactiō est, mendīce homō? **EUC.** Quae rēs?
424	Etiam rogitās? An quia minus quam aequum erat fēcī?

(Euclio threatens Congrio.)

1. **What does Anthrax want to do?** (400)
2. **Why does he rush back into Megadorus' house?** (403–405)
3. **What has happened to Congrio?** (406–411)
4. **What does Euclio intend to do with Congrio?** (416) **Why?** (417)
5. **Does Congrio understand why Euclio is pursuing him?** (423–424)

425 ***sinō, sinere** (3), **sīvī** or **siī, situm**, to allow, let alone. **Sine:** "Stop that!"
   tuō: translate, "to you" or "for you."
   sī hoc caput sentit: "if I have any sense."
426 **quid post sit:** "what may happen later."
   tuum nunc caput sentit: "but your head feels (my blows) now!" Note the play on
      different meanings of **sentit** (425, 426).
427 **quid . . . nam:** = **quidnam**, what, tell me?
428 ***ergō,** therefore, then.
429 **malum** (*interjection added parenthetically to emphasize a question*), the deuce! the
      devil!
430 **utrum . . . an,** whether . . . or. ***crūdus, -a, -um,** uncooked, raw.
   edam: present subjunctive of ***edō, ēsse** (*irreg.*), **ēdī, ēsum,** to eat.
   tūtor, tūtōris (*m*), protector, guardian.
432 **mea:** "my things," "my property." **futūra (esse):** future infinitive of **sum.**
434 **paeniteō, paenitēre** (2), **paenituī,** to cause dissatisfaction, give reason for complaint
      or regret (impersonal, with accusative of the person affected and genitive of the
      thing causing the feeling). **mē haud paenitet (meōrum):** "I am very well satisfied
      with my own things."
   nē: = **nēdum,** still less (is it true that) (+ subjunctive).
   expetō, expetere (3), **expetīvī** or **expetiī, expetītum,** to ask for, seek.
   nē docē: nē is here used with a present imperative to express a prohibition. What is
      the usual construction?
435 **quā . . . grātiā:** "on account of which."
436 **secus** (*adv.*), otherwise, differently.
437 ***angulus, -ī** (*m*), angle, corner.
438 **conclāve, conclāvis** (*n*), room in a house.
   pervium, -ī (*n*), passageway, thoroughfare.
440 **fissilis, -is, -e,** split (**findō, findere,** 3, **fidī, fissum**).
441 **adeō** (*merely reinforcing the* **ut**), to the end that, with the purpose that.
445 **Ita mē bene amet Laverna:** the oath by Laverna emphasizes the declaration that
      follows (**tē . . . tē . . . differam**), "so may Laverna love me, (as) I will defame
      you. . . . "
   Laverna, -ae (*f*), goddess of darkness and thieves. **reddī:** passive infinitive.
446 **pīpulus, -ī** (*m*), shrill or piping sound.
   differō, differre (*irreg.*), **distulī, dīlātum,** to carry in different directions, spread
      abroad, spread bad reports about, defame.
447 **nē,** truly, indeed, assuredly (to be distinguished from the **nē** used in negative pur-
      pose clauses and clauses of fear).
   auspicium, -ī (*n*), augury from the flight of birds, portent or omen of any kind.
448 **medicus, -ī** (*m*), doctor.
   plūs . . . medicō mercēde est opus, "I need more than my pay (just) for the doctor's
      bills."

*This wall painting from Pompeii might be thought to
represent Congrio. Which lines of our play do you think he
would be speaking?*

425	CON.	*(defending himself)* Sine, at hercle cum magnō malō tuō, sī hoc caput
		sentit.
426	EUC.	Pol ego haud sciō quid post sit; *(striking Congrio)* tuum nunc caput sentit.
427		Sed in aedibus quid tibi meīs nam erat negōtī
428		mē absente, nisi ego iusseram? Volō scīre. CON. Tacē ergō.
429		Quia vēnimus coctum ad nūptiās. EUC. Quid tū, malum, cūrās
430		utrum crūdum an coctum ego edam, nisi tū mī es tūtor?
431	CON.	Volō scīre, sinās an nōn sinās nōs coquere hīc cēnam?
432	EUC.	Volō scīre ego item, meae domī meane salva futūra?
433	CON.	Utinam mea mihi modo auferam, quae ad tē tulī, salva:
434		mē haud paenitet, tua nē expetam. EUC. Sciō, nē docē, nōvī.
435	CON.	Quid est quā prohibēs nunc grātiā nōs coquere hīc cēnam?
436		Quid fēcimus, quid dīximus tibi secus quam vellēs?
437	EUC.	Etiam rogitās, sceleste homō, quī angulōs omnīs
438		meārum aedium et conclāvium mihi pervium facitis?
439		Ibi ubi tibi erat negōtium, ad focum sī adessēs,
440		nōn fissile auferrēs caput: meritō id tibi factum est.
441		Adeō ut tū meam sententiam iam nōscere possīs:
442		sī ad iānuam hūc accesseris, nisi iusserō, propius,
443		ego tē faciam miserrimus mortālis ut sīs.
444		Scīs iam meam sententiam. *(Euclio goes back into his house.)* CON.
		(shouting after him) Quō abīs? Redī rūrsus.
445		*(as the doors slam shut)* Ita mē bene amet Laverna, tē iam iam, nisi reddī
446		mihi vāsa iubēs, pīpulō tē hīc differam ante aedīs.
447		*(indignant)* Quid ego nunc agam? Nē ego edepol vēnī hūc
		auspiciō malō. RECITATIVE
448		Nummō sum conductus: plūs iam medicō mercēde est opus.

1. **How does Euclio in line 426 play on Congrio's use of the word** *sentit* **in line 425?**
2. **What does Euclio want to find out from Congrio?** (427–428)
3. **What objection does Euclio make to Congrio's answer?** (429–430)
4. **With what are Congrio and Euclio concerned?** (431–433)
5. **What complaint does Euclio level against Congrio?** (437–438)
6. **What would not have happened if Congrio had been sticking to his business?** (439–440)
7. **What does Euclio now command Congrio to do?** (441–444)
8. **What different purpose than in the past do you think Euclio might have now as he enters his house?** (444)
9. **What does Congrio threaten to do?** (445–446)
10. **On what will Congrio have to spend his pay?** (447–448)

449 ***quōquō**, wherever.
450 **istī** (*adv.*), here.
452 **grex, gregis** (*m*), flock, herd. **vēnālis, vēnālis** (*m*), young slave.
453 **festīnō** (1), to hurry.
454 **temperī**, at the right time, just on time, it's about time.
    *impleō, implēre (2), **implēvī, implētum**, to fill something with something (+ geni-
      tive).
    fustī: ablative. **fissum, -ī** (*n*), cleft, split.
456 **prō** (+ *abl.*), instead of, in return for. ***vapulō** (1), to be beaten.
457 ***dūdum**, just now.
458 **lēge**: from **lēx, lēgis** (*f*), law. **agitō**: future imperative.
    lēge agere, to institute legal proceedings, go to law. **mēcum**: "against me."
    *molestus, -a, -um, troublesome, annoying. **nē sīs**: what kind of a clause?
459 **cruciātus, -ūs** (*m*), an apparatus for torture. **abī in malum cruciātum**: "go to hell!"
    Abī tū modo: supply **in malum cruciātum**; Congrio throws the curse back at Euclio.
460 **illic**: = **ille** + **-ce**; i.e., Congrio.
    incipit: the subject is not **facinus audāx** but **pauper** (461), which is modified by the
      relative clause introduced by **quī** (461).
461 **habēre**: historical infinitive.
462 **velutī**, just as, as for example.
464 **quī surriperent**: relative clause of purpose. **miserō mihi**: dative of separation.
465 **condignē**, in an appropriate manner, fittingly, just as badly.
    *gallinācius, -a, -um, domestic. With **gallus** = a domestic cock.
466 **pecūliāris, -is, -e**, belonging to a person, one's own, personal.
    *paenissimē, very nearly.
467 **scalpurriō, scalpurrīre** (4), to scratch about. **ungula, -ae** (*f*), claw.
468 **circumcircā**, round about, on all sides. ***pectus, pectoris** (*n*), chest, heart.
    peracuō, peracuere (3), **peracuī, peracūtum**, to sharpen, excite thoroughly.
469 **obtruncō** (1), to cut off the head, cut to pieces, slaughter.
    manifestārius, -a, -um, caught in the act.
470 **pollicitōs**: supply **esse**.
471 ***palam facere**, to make known, divulge.
    eximō, eximere (3), **exēmī, exēmptum**, to take out, take away.
    manubrium, -ī (*n*), handle, opportunity.
473 ***affīnis, affīnis** (*m/f*), neighbor.
474 **praetereō, praeterīre** (*irreg.*), **praeterīvī** or **praeteriī, praeteritum**, to pass by, go past.
    quīn (+ *subjunctive*): "but that I should. . . ," "without . . . -ing."
    colloquor, colloquī (3), **collocūtus sum**, to speak with.

*Could this bronze figurine in the Metropolitan Museum of
Art represent Euclio hugging his pot of gold?*

Congrio and his crew linger in front of the house complaining and gesturing until Euclio reappears concealing the pot of gold under his cloak.

EUC. *(aside to himself, as he clutches the pot)*
449   Hoc quidem hercle, quōquō ībō, mēcum erit, mēcum feram,
450   neque istī id in tantīs perīculīs umquam committam ut sit.
451   *(to Congrio and his crew)* Īte sānē nunc intrō omnēs, et coquī et
      tībīcinae.
452   Etiam intrō dūc, sī vīs, vel gregem vēnālium,
453   coquite, facite, festīnāte nunciam quantum libet.
454   CON. *(annoyed)* Temperī, postquam implēvistī fūstī fissōrum caput.
455   EUC. Intrō abī: opera hūc conducta est vestra, nōn ōrātiō.
456   CON. Heus, senex, prō vapulandō hercle ego ab tē mercēdem petam.
457   Coctum ego, nōn vapulātum, dūdum conductus sum.
458   EUC. Lēge agitō mēcum. Molestus nē sīs. Ī cēnam coque,
459   aut abī in malum cruciātum ab aedibus. CON. *(departing with his crew into Euclio's house)* Abī tū modo.
460   EUC. *(alone)* Illic hinc abiit. Dī immortālēs, facinus audāx incipit
461   quī cum opulentō pauper homine rem habēre aut negōtium,
462   velutī Megadōrus temptat mē omnibus miserum modīs,
463   quī simulāvit meī honōris mittere hūc causā coquōs:
464   is eā causā mīsit, hoc *(peeking at the pot under his cloak)* quī surriperent miserō mihi.
465   Condignē etiam meus mē intus gallus gallinācius,
466   quī erat anuī pecūliāris, perdidit paenissimē.
467   Ubi erat haec *(patting the pot)* dēfossa, occēpit ibi scalpurrīre ungulīs
468   circumcircā. Quid opus est verbīs? Ita mī pectus peracuit:
469   capiō fūstem, obtruncō gallum, fūrem manifestārium.
470   Crēdō edepol ego illī mercēdem gallō pollicitōs coquōs,
471   sī id *(looking under his cloak)* palam fēcisset. Exēmī ex manū manubrium.
472   Quid opus est verbīs? Facta est pugna in gallō gallināciō.
      (Megadorus returns at the audience's right from the forum.)
473   Sed Megadōrus meus affinis eccum incēdit ā forō.
474   Iam hunc nōn audeam praeterīre quīn cōnsistam et colloquar.

1. **What does Euclio intend to do with his pot of gold?** (449)
2. **What does Euclio now order Congrio and his crew to do?** (451–453)
3. **About what does Congrio continue to complain?** (454–457)
4. **How does Euclio feel about his new relationship with his rich neighbor?** (460–461)
5. **Whom does he consider responsible for the trouble the relationship is causing, himself or Megadorus?** (462)
6. **With what does Euclio charge Megadorus in line 463?**
7. **For what reason does Euclio claim that Megadorus really sent the cooks?** (464)
8. **Why was Euclio frightened by the behavior of the cock?** (465–467)
9. **Why did Euclio kill the cock?** (469)
10. **What does Euclio think the cooks had to do with the cock?** (470–471)
11. **What does Euclio mean by the proverbial statement *Exēmī ex manū manubrium?*** (471)

475 **nārrō** (1), to relate, tell.
477 **sapienter**, wisely. Supply **dīcunt . . . esse.**
478 **meō . . . animō**: "in my judgment."
480 *****indōtātus, -a, -um**, not provided with a dowry (**dōs, dōtis**, *f*).
481 **concors, concordis**, agreeing in feeling and opinion, harmonious.
482 **invidia, -ae** (*f*), envy. **ūtāmur**: "we should experience."
483 *****malam rem**: i.e., punishment.
485 **In maximam . . . populī partem**: "For the majority of the people." **illuc**: = **illud** +
    -ce.
486 **altercātiō, altercātiōnis** (*f*), dispute, wrangle, altercation, contention directed against
    someone (**in** + *acc.*).
487 **insatietās, insatietātis** (*f*), insatiate desire, greediness.
488 *****sūtor, sūtōris** (*m*), shoemaker, cobbler.
    capere est quī possit modum: = **est quī possit modum capere. modum capere** (+
    dat.), to set a limit or bounds to.
489 **quī**: supply **eī** as antecedent, "to him who should say this ("**Quō . . . pōnitur?**"), (I
    would reply). . . . " Megadorus' reply is contained in line 491.
    Quō: "Where," "With whom."
491 **libeant**: personal, "they may wish." **nūbant**: jussive subjunctive.
    dum . . . nē: "provided that . . . not."
    comes, comitis (*m/f*), companion, something that goes along with someone.
493 **parent**: subjunctive of **parō** (1).
    prō (+ *abl.*), instead of.
    quōs ferant: "which they would bring (to their husbands)." The antecedent of **quōs**
    is **mōrēs** (492).
    quam: "than," following **meliōrēs** (492).
494 **faciam**: "I would suppose."
    *****mūlus, -ī** (*m*), mule. Ladies of rank had their carriages drawn by mules, which
    therefore became very expensive. *****pretium, -ī** (*n*), price, value.
495 *****vīlis, -is, -e**, cheap. **Gallicus, -a, -um**, of Gaul (modern France), Gallic.
    canthērius, -ī (*m*) (*Greek loan word*), horse (usually of poor quality), hack, nag.
496 **Ita . . . ut**: for the construction, see the note on line 445.
497 **lepidē**, charmingly, pleasantly. **ad** (+ *acc.*), (here) for, in support of.
    parsimōnia, -ae (*f*), thrift, frugality, economy, niggardliness.
500 **enim**: = **enimvērō**, certainly, to be sure, of course.
501 **ancilla, -ae** (*f*), a female slave. **mūliō, mūliōnis** (*m*), a mule-driver.
    pedisequus, -ī (*m*), a male attendant, manservant.
502 **salūtigerulus, -a, -um**, employed to carry salutations.
    quī (*adverbial abl.*), by which means, whereby, wherewith.
503 *****mātrōna, -ae** (*f*), married woman, matron.
    pernōscō, pernōscere (3), **pernōvī, pernōtum**, to become thoroughly acquainted with,
    (perfect) to be thoroughly conversant with.
    *****probē**, properly, well.
504 **Mōribus praefectum mulierum**: such overseers of women's characters existed in
    several Greek states, including Athens and Sparta.
    factum: supply **esse; factum esse** = **fierī**, "to be made."

As Megadorus returns from the forum, his attention is fixed on his ideas about marriage, and, not seeing Euclio, who listens with fascination, he delivers himself of a graphic soliloquy on the extravagances of a well-dowered wife.

475	**MEG.** Nārrāvī amīcīs multīs cōnsilium meum	DIALOGUE
476	dē condiciōne hāc. Eucliōnis fīliam	
477	laudant. Sapienter factum et cōnsiliō bonō.	
478	Nam meō quidem animō sī idem faciant cēterī	
479	opulentiōrēs, pauperiōrum fīliās	
480	ut indōtātās dūcant uxōrēs domum,	
481	et multō fīat cīvitās concordior,	
482	et invidiā nōs minōre ūtāmur quam ūtimur,	
483	et illae malam rem metuant quam metuunt magis,	
484	et nōs minōre sumptū sīmus quam sumus.	
485	In maximam illuc populī partem est optimum;	
486	in pauciōrēs avidōs altercātiō est,	
487	quōrum animīs avidīs atque īnsatiētātibus	
488	neque lēx neque sūtor capere est quī possit modum.	
489	Namque hōc quī dīcat, "Quō illae nūbent dīvitēs	
490	dōtātae, sī istuc iūs pauperibus pōnitur?"	
491	Quō libeant nūbant, dum dōs nē fīat comes.	
492	Hoc sī ita fīat, mōrēs meliōrēs sibi	
493	parent, prō dōte quōs ferant, quam nunc ferunt;	
494	ego faciam mūlī, pretiō quī superant equōs,	
495	sint vīliōrēs Gallicīs canthēriīs.	
496	**EUC.** *(aside, approvingly)* Ita mē dī amābunt ut ego hunc auscultō libēns.	
497	Nimis lepidē fēcit verba ad parsimōniam.	
498	**MEG.** *(continuing his soliloquy)* Nūlla igitur dīcat, "Equidem dōtem ad tē attulī	
499	maiōrem multō quam tibi erat pecūnia;	
500	enim mihi quidem aequum est purpuram atque aurum darī,	
501	ancillās, mūlōs, mūliōnēs, pedisequōs,	
502	salūtigerulōs puerōs, vehicula quī vehar."	
503	**EUC.** *(aside, with a smile and chuckle)* Ut mātrōnārum hic facta pernōvit probē!	
504	Mōribus praefectum mulierum hunc factum velim.	

1. **What has Megadorus been doing, and with what result?** (475–477)
2. **What novel social custom does Megadorus propose?** (478–480)
3. **What four advantages would it have?** (481–484)
4. **For what portion of the population would his plan be good?** (485)
5. **Who would object to it?** (486–488)
6. **What would rich women do if Megadorus' novel proposal were adopted?** (489–491)
7. **How would this make rich women change for the better?** (492–493)
8. **What other result would Megadorus' proposal have?** (494–495)
9. **What pleases Euclio about what he hears?** (496–497)
10. **What is the problem with women whose dowries are larger than their husbands' assets?** (498–502)

43

505 **plaustrum, -ī** (*n*), wagon, cart.
506 **rūs, rūris** (*n*), the country. **rūrī**, in the country.
507 **praequam**, compared with. **sūmptūs petunt**: i.e., come to the rich lady's house for payment of services rendered. The subject of **petunt** is defined in the following lines.
508 *****fullō, fullōnis** (*m*), fuller, launderer.
    phrygiō, phrygiōnis (*m*), embroiderer (the Phrygians, a people living in Asia Minor, supposedly invented embroidery). **aurifex, aurificis** (*m*), goldsmith.
    lānārius, -ī (*m*), worker or dealer in wool (**lāna, -ae,** *f*).
509 **caupō, caupōnis** (*m*), shopkeeper.
    patagiārius, -a, -um, dealing in **patagia** (**patagium, -ī,** *n*, border on a woman's tunic).
    indusiārius, -ī (*m*), maker or seller of **indusia** (**indusium, -ī,** *n*, outer tunic).
510 **flammārius, -ī** (*m*), one who dyes garments flame-colored.
    violārius, -ī (*m*), one who dyes garments violet-colored.
    carinārius, -ī (*m*), one who dyes garments brown.
511 **manuleārius, -ī** (*m*), maker of sleeved garments (**manuleus, -ī,** *m*, long sleeve).
    murobathārius, -ī (*m*), (meaning unknown; the text may be corrupt here).
512 **propōla, -ae** (*m*) (*Greek loan word*), retailer. **linteō, linteōnis** (*m*), weaver or dealer in linen (**linteum, -ī,** *n*). **calceolārius, -ī** (*m*), shoemaker (**calceus, -ī,** *m*, shoe).
513 **sedentārius, -a, -um**, sedentary, sitting.
    diabathrārius, -ī (*m*), maker of **diabathra** (**diabathrum, -ī,** *n*, *Greek loan word*, a slipper).
514 **soleārius, -ī** (*m*), sandal-maker (**solea, -ae,** *f*, sandal).
    molocinārius, -ī (*m*), maker or seller of mallow-colored garments (**molochē, -ēs,** *f*, *Greek loan word*, mallow).
515 **sarcinātor, sarcinātōris** (*m*), a mender of clothes (**sarciō, sarcīre,** 4, to mend).
516 **strophārius, -ī** (*m*), maker or seller of **strophia** (*****strophium, -ī,** *n*, *Greek loan word*, band worn by women under the breasts). *****simul**, at the same time, together.
    zōnārius, -ī (*m*), maker or seller of girdles (**zōna, -ae,** *f*, *Greek loan word*, belt, girdle).
517 **hōsce**: = **hōs** + **-ce**. *****absolvō, absolvere** (3), **absolvī, absolūtum**, to release, pay off. **cēdunt**: = **incēdunt**.
518 **trecēnī, -ae, -a** (*a distributive adjective*), three hundred each.
    phylacista, -ae (*m*) (*Greek loan word*), jailer (used comically of a creditor who duns for his money and makes a prisoner of the debtor by keeping watch on his house. The text may be corrupt here; some editors read **thylacistae**, a rare Greek word for "beggars").
    ātrium, -ī (*n*), the main room in a Roman-style house, where callers were received.
519 **textor, textōris** (*m*), weaver. **limbulārius, a, -um**, concerned with making ornamental hems or fringes (**limbus, -ī,** *m*, ornamental border, fringe).
    arculārius, -ī (*m*), maker of chests or boxes (**arca, -ae,** *f*, chest, box).
521 **īnfector, īnfectōris** (*m*), dyer (**īnficiō, īnficere,** 3, **īnfēcī, īnfectum**, to immerse in a pigment, dye). **crocōtārius, -a, -um**, concerned with saffron-colored robes (*****crocōta, -ae,** *f*, saffron-colored robe worn by women).
522 **aliqua mala crux**: "some other tormenter."
523 **compellō** (1), to address, speak to.
    dēsinō, dēsinere (3), **dēsīvī** or **dēsiī, dēsitum**, to leave off, stop.
525 **nūgigerulus, -ī** (*m*), one who peddles worthless articles (**nūgae, -ārum,** *f pl*, idle talk, worthless stuff, trash). **rēs**: i.e., money.
    solvō, solvere (3), **solvī, solūtum**, to loosen, untie, settle (a debt). **rem solvere**: to settle up, make payment.
526 **postrēmus, -a, -um**, last, final. **ad postrēmum**, finally. **cēdit**: = **incēdit**.
    mīles: the soldier comes to collect the tax to support the army or perhaps to beg.
527 **Ītur**(*impersonal*): "There is a going," "You go" (i.e., to your banker).
    ratiōnem putāre, to add up and balance, an account. *****argentārius, -ī** (*m*), banker.
528 **imprānsus, -a, -um**, not having had one's morning meal (**prandeō, prandēre** 2, **prandī, prānsum**, to eat one's morning or midday meal). **darī**: = **fore ut dētur**, "that it will be given."
529 **disputō** (1), to argue one's case, argue out.
530 **ipse**: = **dominus**.
531 **prōrogō** (1), to extend, postpone.
532 **haec**: = **hae** (fem. nom. pl.) + **-ce**.
533 **incommoditās, incommoditātis** (*f*), inconvenience. **intolerābilis, -is, -e**, unendurable.
535 **mactō** (1), to honor, afflict, punish with (+ ablative). *****damnum, -ī** (*n*), financial loss.

505	**MEG.** *(continuing his soliloquy)* Nunc quōquō veniās plūs plaustrōrum in aedibus
506	videās quam rūrī, quandō ad vīllam vēneris.
507	Sed hoc etiam pulchrum est praequam ubi sūmptūs petunt.
508	Stat fullō, phrygiō, aurifex, lānārius;
509	caupōnēs patagiāriī, indusiāriī,
510	flammāriī, violāriī, carināriī;
511	aut manuleāriī, aut murobathāriī,
512	propōlae linteōnēs, calceolāriī;
513	sedentāriī sūtōrēs diabathrāriī,
514	soleāriī astant, astant molocināriī;
515	petunt fullōnēs, sarcinātōrēs petunt;
516	strophiāriī astant, astant simul zōnāriī.
517	Iam hōsce absolūtōs cēnseās: cēdunt, petunt
518	trecēnī, cum stant phylacistae in ātriīs
519	textōrēs limbulāriī, arculāriī.
520	Ducuntur, datur aes. Iam absolūtōs cēnseās,
521	cum incēdunt īnfectōrēs crocōtāriī,
522	aut aliqua mala crux semper est quae aliquid petat.
523	**EUC.** *(aside, with obvious relish)* Compellārem ego illum, nisi metuam nē dēsinat
524	memorāre mōrēs mulierum; nunc sīc sinam.
525	**MEG.** *(continuing his soliloquy)* Ubi nūgigerulīs rēs solūta est omnibus,
526	ibi ad postrēmum cēdit mīles, aes petit.
527	Ītur, putātur ratiō cum argentāriō;
528	mīles imprānsus astat, aes cēnset darī.
529	Ubi disputāta est ratiō cum argentāriō,
530	etiam ipse ultrō dēbet argentāriō;
531	spēs prōrogātur mīlitī in alium diem.
532	Haec sunt atque aliae multae in magnīs dōtibus
533	incommoditātēs sūmptūsque intolerābilēs.
534	Nam quae indōtāta est, ea in potestāte est virī;
535	dōtātae mactant et malō et damnō virōs.

1. **What has women's extravagance made more prevalent in the city than in the country?** (505–506)
2. **On what kinds of things do well-dowered wives spend the household's money?** (507–516) **How would you categorize them?**
3. **Why are so many of the words in this list** (508–516) **of Greek origin?**
4. **Who pays off the creditors, the wife or the husband?** (517, 520) **What feelings are suggested by the repetition of the phrase** *iam . . . absolūtōs cēnseās* **in 517 and 520?**
5. **How is the soldier different from the others who come to the household?** (525–526)
6. **Where does the master of the household have to go now that all the creditors have been paid off?** (527)
7. **Why doesn't the soldier get any money?** (530)
8. **How does Megadorus feel about all of this?** (532–533)
9. **What is the advantage of a wife without dowry?** (534)

537 **nimium**, too much, extremely.
  libenter, with pleasure, gladly.
  ēdī: from **edō, ēsse** (*irreg.*), **ēdī, ēsum**, to eat.
  sermō, sermōnis (*m*), speech, talk.
538 **an** (*introducing direct questions, with the notion of surprise*), can it really be that?
  prīncipium, -ī (*n*), beginning.
539 **aliquantō**, to some extent, somewhat, considerably.
540 **nitidus, -a, -um**, bright, elegant, well-groomed.
541 **prō** (+ *abl.*), in proportion to.
  nitor, nitōris (*m*), brightness, elegance, style.
  glōria, -ae (*f*), (here) show, pomp.
542 **oriundus, -a, -um**, descended from.
544 **opīniōne melius**: "any better than people think."
  rēs: i.e., "wealth," "fortune."
  struō, struere (3), **strūxī, strūctum**, to pile up.
545 **Immō est**: supply **tibi** (dative of possession).
546 **sōspitō** (1), to save, protect.
549 **senātū**: here used figuratively of the conversation in which the two men are engaged.
  sēvocō (1), to call away. **sē sēvocāre**, to separate oneself.
550 **meditor, meditārī** (1), **meditātus sum**, to have in mind, intend.
551 **Quī**: i.e., "You who. . . ."
553 **quīngentī, -ae, -a**, five hundred.
554 **sēnī, -ae, -a**, six apiece.
  Gēryonāceus, -a, -um, of or belonging to Geryon, a mythical three-bodied monster who lived in Erythea, an island in the far West. **genere Gēryonāceō**: ablative of description, "of the race of Geryon."
555 **Argus, -ī** (*m*), the guardian with a hundred eyes sent by Juno to keep watch over Io and later killed by Mercury. **oculeus, -a, -um**, made or consisting of eyes.
556 **quondam**, formerly, once upon a time.
  Iō, (*dat.*) **Iōnī** (*f*), the daughter of Inachus who was loved by Zeus and subsequently metamorphosed into a cow.
  ***Iūnō, Iūnōnis** (*f*), Juno, the wife of Jupiter and queen of the gods.
  addō, addere (3), **addidī, additum**, to attach to, put along with.
558 **interbibō, interbibere** (3), to drink dry, drain.
  scatō, scatere (3) (+ *abl.*), to gush with. The subject of **scatat** is **Corinthiēnsis fōns Pīrēnē**, to be supplied from the following line.
559 **Corinthiēnsis, -is, -e**, Corinthian. **fōns, fontis** (*m*), spring of water.
  Pīrēnē, Pīrēnēs (*Latin acc.* **Pīrēnam**) (*f*) (*Greek loan word*), a spring or fountain in Corinth associated with Pegasus and the Muses.

This painting from a fifth century B.C. Greek vase shows something of the sumptuous elegance that Megadorus mocks. The figure at the far right is the mythical Alcestis as a bride.

MEG. *(his eye finally falling on Euclio)*
536   Sed eccum affīnem ante aedīs. Quid agis, Eucliō?
537 EUC. Nimium libenter ēdī sermōnem tuum.
538 MEG. An audīvistī? EUC. Usque ā prīncipiō omnia.
    MEG. *(eyeing Euclio's shabby and unkempt appearance)*
539   Tamen meō quidem animō aliquantō faciās rēctius,
540   sī nitidior sīs fīliae nūptiīs.
541 EUC. *(whining)* Prō rē nitōrem et glōriam prō cōpiā
542   quī habent, meminērunt sēsē unde oriundī sint.
543   Neque pol, Megadōre, mihi neque cuiquam pauperī
544   opīniōne melius rēs strūcta est domī *(clutching the pot tightly)*.
545 MEG. *(pleasantly)* Immō est quod satis est, et dī faciant ut sit
546   plūs plūsque et istuc sōspitent quod nunc habēs.
547 EUC. *(to himself, in some alarm)* Illud mihi verbum nōn placet, "quod nunc habēs."
548   Tam hōc scit mē habēre quam ego. Anus fēcit palam.
549 MEG. Quid tū tē sōlus ē senātū sēvocās?
550 EUC. Pol ego tē ut accūsem meritō meditābar. MEG. Quid est?
551 EUC. Quid sit mē rogitās? Quī mihi omnīs angulōs
552   fūrum implēvistī in aedibus miserō mihi,
553   quī mī intrō mīsistī in aedīs quīngentōs coquōs
554   cum sēnīs manibus, genere Gēryonāceō;
555   quōs sī Argus servet, quī oculeus tōtus fuit,
556   quem quondam Iōnī Iūnō custōdem addidit,
557   is numquam servet. Praetereā tībīcinam,
558   quae mī interbibere sōla, sī vīnō scatat,
559   Corinthiēnsem fontem Pīrēnam potest.
560   Tum obsōnium autem— MEG. *(interrupting)* Pol vel legiōnī satis est.

1. How did Euclio feel about Megadorus' speech? (537)
2. What suggestion does Megadorus make to Euclio? (539–540)
3. How does Euclio excuse his shabby appearance? (541–544)
4. How does Megadorus regard Euclio's financial position? (545–546)
5. What suspicion does Megadorus' comment arouse in Euclio? (547–548)
6. How does Euclio explain the lapse in conversation? (550)
7. What three accusations does Euclio bring against Megadorus? (551–560)
8. What does Euclio call the cooks? (552)
9. How does Euclio exaggerate in describing the cooks? (553–554)
10. Why is it surprising that Argus would not be able to guard the cooks? (555–557)
11. What, according to Euclio, is the claim to fame of the *tībīcina*? (557–559)

562 **cūriōsus, -a, -um**, careful, curious, careworn. Euclio, worried about his buried treasure, seems to be concerned that the lamb is too "curious." In line 563 Megadorus, not understanding what Euclio is worried about, asks, perhaps facetiously,
how a lamb could be a priest (**cūriō**), implying that Euclio's adjective **cūriōsam**
meant "priestly." In line 564 Euclio carefully covers up his reference to the lamb's
excessive "curiosity" by suggesting that what he meant was that the lamb is
"careworn" (**cūrā macet**) and thus reduced to skin and bones.

    bēlua, -ae (f), beast, wild animal.

563 **quī** (adv.), in what way? how?

    cūriō, cūriōnis (m), the title of a priest, apparently presiding over a **cūria** (one of the
thirty divisions of the Roman people, a voting ward).

564 **os, ossis** (n), bone. **pellis, pellis** (f), skin, hide.

    maceō, macēre (2), to be thin.

565 **exta, -ōrum** (n pl), the internal organs of an animal. **eī vīvō**: dative of reference,
"while he's still alive."

566 **pellūceō, pellūcēre** (2), to transmit light, be transparent.

    lanterna, -ae (f), a lantern (made from horn cut into thin sheets).

    Pūnicus, -a, -um, Punic, Carthaginian.

568 ***efferō, efferre** (irreg.), **extulī, ēlātum**, to carry out, carry out for burial. (**ut**) **locēs
efferendum**: "that you arrange for the lamb's funeral." Cf. the phrase **fūnus locāre**,
to contract with an undertaker about a funeral.

    mortuus, -a, -um, dead.

569 ***pōtō** (1), to drink.

570 **iusserō**: = simply **iubēbō**.

571 **cadus, -ī** (m) (Greek loan word), large jar of wine. **ā mē**: = **ā meā domō**.

573 **madidus, -a, -um**, wet, drenched, drunk.

574 **tibi cui**: we would expect **tē** instead of **tibi**, but the **tē** is attracted into the case of
the relative pronoun, **cui**.

575 **dēpōnō, dēpōnere** (3), **dēposuī, dēpositum**, to put down, lay a body to rest.

    affectō (1), to try to reach or achieve, (with **viam**) to attempt.

576 **post** (adv.), afterwards. **hoc**: i.e., the pot of gold, subject of **commūtet**.

    commūtō (1), to change.

    colōnia, -ae (f), settlement or colony of citizens sent from Rome, dwelling place
away from home.

577 **alicubi**, elsewhere.

    ***abstrūdō, abstrūdere** (3), **abstrūsī, abstrūsum**, to conceal from view, hide.

578 **perdiderit**: future perfect indicative used paratactically instead of a subjunctive introduced by **ut** in a substantive clause of result ("I'll see that he loses. . .").

579 **sacrificō** (1), to perform a sacrifice (here in preparation for the wedding).

580 **nē** (affirmative particle), truly, indeed, assuredly.

582 **factū**: ablative supine of **faciō, facere** (3), **fēcī, factum**; with **optimum**.

583 **Fideī**: the Roman goddess Fides was associated with Jupiter and worshiped in a
temple on the Capitoline Hill, thought to have been built by Numa. Her festival
was celebrated on 1 October.

    ***fānum, -ī** (n), shrine.

584 **sīs**: = **sī vīs**.

585 **immūtō** (1), to change. **nē tū immūtāveris nōmen**: perfect subjunctive in a prohibition; i.e., "do not allow yourself to be called **īnfida**." **concrēdam**: present subjunctive.

586 **frētus, -a, -um** (+ abl.), relying on. **fidūcia, -ae** (f), trust, confidence. Note the alliteration.

48

561	MEG. Etiam agnum mīsī. EUC. Quō quidem agnō satis sciō
562	magis cūriōsam nusquam esse ūllam bēluam.
563	MEG. Volō ego ex tē scīre quī sit agnus cūriō.
	EUC. *(laughing and pleased with his own wit)*
564	Quia ossa ac pellis tōtus est, ita cūrā macet.
565	Quīn exta īnspicere in sōle eī vīvō licet:
566	ita is pellūcet quasi lanterna Pūnica.
567	MEG. Caedendum condūxī ego illum. EUC. Tum tū īdem optimum est
568	locēs efferendum; nam iam, crēdō, mortuus est.
	MEG. *(ignoring Euclio's sarcasm and determined to maintain cheerful relations)*
569	Pōtāre ego hodiē, Euclio, tēcum volō.
570	EUC. *(gruffly)* Nōn pōtem ego quidem hercle. MEG. At ego iusserō
571	cadum ūnum vīnī veteris ā mē afferrī.
572	EUC. Nōlō hercle, nam mihi bibere dēcrētum est aquam.
573	MEG. *(jovially)* Ego tē hodiē reddam madidum, sī vīvō, probē,
574	tibi cui dēcrētum est bibere aquam. EUC. *(aside)* Sciō quam rem agat:
575	ut mē dēpōnat vīnō, eam affectat viam,
576	post hoc quod habeō ut commūtet colōniam.
577	Ego id cavēbō, nam alicubi abstrūdam forīs.
578	Ego faciam et operam et vīnum perdiderit simul.
579	MEG. Ego, nisi quid mē vīs, eō lavātum, ut sacrificem.
	(In good spirits and joyful anticipation, Megadorus goes into his house.)
	EUC. *(alone; looking under his cloak and patting the pot affectionately)*
580	Edepol nē tū, aula, multōs inimīcōs habēs
581	atque istuc aurum quod tibi concrēditum est.
582	Nunc hoc mihi factū est optimum, ut tē auferam,
583	aula, in Fideī fānum. *(going over to the temple of Fides on the left)* Ibi
	abstrūdam probē.
584	Fidēs, nōvistī mē et ego tē: cavē sīs tibi
585	nē tū immūtāveris nōmen, sī hoc concrēdam.
586	Ībō ad tē frētus tuā, Fidēs, fidūciā.
	(Euclio takes the pot into the temple.)

1. Why does Euclio find the lamb that Megadorus sent objectionable? (562)
2. Why does Euclio change the subject from the lamb's curiosity to its emaciation when he offers his explanation in lines 564–566?
3. To what does he compare the lamb? (566)
4. What is the only thing that the lamb is good for, according to Euclio? (567–568)
5. What does Megadorus offer for the occasion? (569)
6. Why do you think that Euclio on this occasion feels he must reject Megadorus' offer? (572)
7. How does Megadorus' response (573–574) confirm Euclio's suspicion?
8. What does Euclio now decide to do with the pot of gold? (577) What had he intended to do with it earlier? (449)
9. What seems particularly appropriate about the place where Euclio decides to hide the pot of gold? (584–586)

587 *frūgī (*indeclinable adjective*), having merit or worth, honest, deserving.
   *persequor, persequī (3), persecūtus sum, to follow persistently, pursue.
588 molestia, -ae (*f*), trouble, annoyance. morae molestiaeque: datives of purpose after nē
   . . . habeat, "that he not consider. . . ."
589 quī . . . servus: = servus quī.
   ex sententiā: "to his (i.e., his master's) satisfaction."
   postulat: here, "expects," "wishes."
590 in erum: "for (his) master."
   matūrus, -a, -um, mature, timely, speedy. sērus, -a, -um, late, slow, tardy.
   condecet, condecēre (2) (*impersonal*), it is fitting.
   capessō, capessere (3), capessīvī or capessiī, to seize, enter on, engage in.
591 sīn, if however, but if.
   dormītō (1), to feel sleepy, allow one's energy or attention to flag, sleep.
(592) Lines 592 to 598 are thought to be an interpolation introduced in a later production
   of the play and are omitted from this text.
599 ēdiscō, ēdiscere (3), ēdidicī, to get to know thoroughly, learn thoroughly.
   frōns: i.e., of the master. oculī: i.e., of the slave.
600 citus, -a, -um, moving quickly. quadrīga, -ae (*f*), four-horse chariot.
601 abstineō, abstinēre (2), abstinuī, abstentum (+ *abl.*), to keep away from, avoid.
   cēnsiō, cēnsiōnis (*f*), punishment (imposed by a censor).
   būbulus, -a, -um, of or belonging to a bull, cow, or ox (used frequently of a whip
   made from oxhide).
602 redigō, redigere (2), redēgī, redāctum, to bring back, restore.
   splendor, splendōris (*m*), sheen, brightness.
   compes, compedis (*f*), shackles for the feet, fetters. compedīs: = compedēs. rediget
   . . . in splendōrem compedīs: "shine up shackles."
603 huius: i.e., of this Euclio who lives here.
604 *renūntiō (1), to report, announce.
605 speculor, speculārī (1), speculātus sum, to spy out, watch.
   particeps, participis (*m/f*), a participant, sharer of or in (+ genitive). quae fierent:
   this clause serves as the genitive complement of particeps, "so that he might
   share in (knowledge of) what is happening."
606 sine omnī: = sine ūllā. suscīpiō, suscīpiōnis (*f*), suspicion. āra, -ae (*f*), altar.
   assīdō, assīdere (3), assēdī, to sit down. sacer, sacra, sacrum, sacred.
607 arbitrārī, (here) to observe, witness.
608 indicāveris: perfect subjunctive in a prohibition.
609 latebra, -ae (*f*), hiding place.
   *situs, -a, -um, laid up, stored, deposited.
610 nē, truly, indeed, assuredly. illic: = ille + -ce.
612 dīvīnus, -a, -um, divine. rēs dīvīna, a religious rite.
613 arcessō, arcessere (3), arcessīvī or arcessiī, arcessītum, to fetch, summon, invite.
   arcessat: subjunctive by assimilation to dūcat.
   extemplō: with dūcat.
614 etiam atque etiam, more and more, earnestly. Supply ōrō, "I beg you."
615 *lūcus, -ī (*m*), sacred grove.

The stage is empty for a few moments. A slave belonging to Lyconides appears (Lyconidis servus = L.S.), making his way carefully along the street from the forum; as he reaches the altar, he complacently announces himself, his mission, and his code of behavior to the audience.

587	**L.S.**	Hoc est servī facinus frūgī, facere quod ego persequor, RECITATIVE
588		nē morae molestiaeque imperium erīle habeat sibi.
589		Nam quī erō ex sententiā servīre servus postulat,
590		in erum matūra, in sē sēra condecet capessere.
591		Sīn dormitet, ita dormitet servum sēsē ut cōgitet.
599		Erī ille imperium ēdiscat, ut quod frōns velit oculī sciant;
600		quod iubeat citīs quadrīgīs citius properet persequī.
601		Quī ea cūrābit abstinēbit cēnsiōne būbulā,
602		nec suā operā rediget umquam in splendōrem compedīs.
603		Nunc erus meus amat fīliam huius Eucliōnis pauperis;
604		eam erō nunc renūntiātum est nūptum huic Megadōrō darī.
605		Is speculātum hūc mīsit mē, ut quae fierent fieret particeps.
		(sitting down on the altar of Apollo)
606		Nunc sine omnī suspīciōne in ārā hīc assīdam sacrā;
607		hinc ego et hūc et illūc poterō quid agant arbitrārī.
		(Euclio emerges from the temple of Fides, not noticing the slave, and plaintively invokes Fides.)
608	**EUC.**	Tū modo cavē cuiquam indicāveris aurum meum esse istīc, Fidēs:
609		nōn metuō nē quisquam inveniat, ita probē in latebrīs situm est.
610		Edepol nē illic pulchram praedam agat, sī quis illam invēnerit
611		aulam onustam aurī; vērum id tē quaesō ut prohibeās, Fidēs.
612		*(going toward his house)* Nunc lavābō, ut rem dīvīnam faciam, nē affīnem morer
613		quīn ubi arcessat meam extemplō fīliam dūcat domum.
		(looking back at the temple of Fides)
614		Vidē, Fidēs, etiam atque etiam nunc, salvam ut aulam ab tē auferam:
615		tuae fideī concrēdidī aurum, in tuō lūcō et fānō est situm.
		(Euclio goes into his house, still not noticing the slave.)

1. **What opinion does the slave of Lyconides have of himself?** (587–588) **How does he regard his master's commands?** (588)
2. **Whom should a good slave put first, his master or himself?** (589–590)
3. **How should a good slave sleep?** (591)
4. **How should a good slave learn his master's will?** (599)
5. **How will the good slave be rewarded?** (601–602)
6. **With whom is the slave's master in love?** (603)
7. **What has Lyconides just learned?** (604)
8. **Why did Lyconides send his slave here?** (605)
9. **Why does the slave sit on the altar of Apollo?** (606–607)
10. **What precaution did Euclio take in hiding his gold in the temple?** (609)
11. **What does Euclio propose to do now?** (612) **Why?** (612–613)

616 **quod**: with **facinus**.
618 **fidēlis, -is, -e**, faithful.
619 **huius**: i.e., Phaedria. Word order: **huius quam erus meus amat**.
620 *****perscrūtor, perscrūtārī** (1), **perscrūtātus sum**, to examine a place to find something hidden.
    uspiam, anywhere, somewhere.
621 **occupātus, -a, -um**, busy.
622 **mulsum -ī** (*n*), a drink made from honey and wine.
    congiālis, -is, -e, holding a **congius** (**congius, -ī,** *m*, a liquid measure equivalent to 1/8 of an amphora or 6 pints). *****plēnus, -a, -um**, full.   **faciam**: "dedicate."
    fidēlia, -ae (*f*), large pot, pail, bucket. Note the pun on **Fidēs** and **fidēlis**.
624 **temerē**, by chance, by accident.   *****corvus, -ī** (*m*), raven.
    cantō (1), to sing, (of birds) sing, call.
    *****laevus, -a, -um**, left. A raven on the left was an unlucky omen.
625 **rādō, rādere** (3), **rāsī, rāsum**, to scrape, scratch.
    crocciō, croccīre (4), to croak (used of ravens).
626 **ars, artis** (*f*), art, an artistic performance.
    lūdicrus, -a, -um, playful, lighthearted, of or relating to the stage, theatrical. **ars lūdicra**, a theatrical performance (including those forms of entertainment like the mime which featured dancing). **artem lūdicram facere**, to dance.
627 **ēmicō** (1), to make a sudden movement forward, outward, or upward, (of the heart) give a jump.
    Sed ego cessō currere: cf. line 397.
628 **lumbrīcus, -ī** (*m*), earthworm.   **ērepō, ērepere** (3), **ērepsī**, to creep or crawl out.
629 *****nusquam**, nowhere.
    compāreō, compārēre (2), **compāruī**, to be able to be seen, be in evidence.
    peris: present tense where we would expect the future **perībis**.
630 **praestrīgiātor, praestrīgiātoris** (*m*), trickster (**prestrīgia, -ae,** *f*, trick).
631 *****agitō** (1), to move, stir, agitate.
    commercium, -ī (*n*), trade, business, dealings, relationship. **commercī**: partitive genitive with **quid**.
632 **afflictō** (1), to strike repeatedly, knock about.
    raptō (1), to carry away forcibly, drag violently off.
633 **verberābilis, -is, -e**, worthy of a beating.
    trifūr, trifūris (*m*), triple thief.
634 **sīs**: = **sī vīs**.
635 **tibi**: L.S. means "from you"; Euc. means "for you(rself)."   **cedo** (*imperative*): give! hand over!
636 **Ecquid agis**: an impatient question, "You gonna do it?"
637 **Pōne**: imperative of **pōnō, pōnere**. The slave of Lyconides interprets it obscenely as **pōne** (*adv.*), in the rear, behind.
    datō (1), to be in the habit or practice of giving (here in an obscene sense).
    cōnsuētus, -a, -um, accustomed to, used to.
638 **hōc**: = **hūc**. **sīs**: = **sī vīs**.
    cavilla, -ae (*f*), jesting, banter.
    *****nūgae, -ārum** (*f pl*), idle talk, nonsense. *****nūgās agere**, to waste one's efforts, joke, jest, fool around.

52

L.S. *(leaping up in excitement)*

616 Dī immortālēs, quod ego hunc hominem facinus audīvī loquī?
617 Sē aulam onustam aurī abstrūsisse hīc intus in fānō Fideī.
618 Cavē tū illī fidēlis, quaesō, potius fueris quam mihi.
619 Atque hic pater est, ut ego opīnor, huius erus quam amat meus.
(going toward the temple)
620 Ībō hinc intrō, perscrūtābor fānum, sī inveniam uspiam
621 aurum, dum hic est occupātus. Sed sī reppererō, ō Fidēs,
622 mulsī congiālem plēnam faciam tibi fidēliam.
623 Id adeō tibi faciam; vērum ego mihi bibam, ubi id fēcerō.

The slave of Lyconides runs into the temple; at the same moment the cawing of a raven is heard and Euclio rushes out of his house in a panic.

624 EUC. Nōn temerē est quod corvus cantat mihi nunc ab laevā manū;
625 simul rādēbat pedibus terram et vōce crocciēbat suā:
626 continuō meum cor coepit artem facere lūdicram
627 atque in pectus ēmicāre. Sed ego cessō currere?

Euclio dashes into the temple; loud cries and the sounds of a scuffle are heard within the temple; the slave of Lyconides emerges, followed by Euclio in pursuit.

628 EUC. Ī forās, lumbrīce, quī sub terrā ērepsistī modo,
629 quī modo nusquam compārēbās, nunc cum compārēs peris.
630 Edepol tē, praestrīgiātor, miserīs iam accipiam modīs.
631 L.S. Quae tē mala crux agitat? Quid tibi mēcum est commercī, senex?
632 Quid mē afflictās? Quid mē raptās? Quā mē causā verberās?
EUC. *(giving him three blows in quick succession)*
633 Verberābilissime, etiam rōgitās, nōn fūr, sed trifūr?
634 L.S. Quid tibi surripuī? EUC. Redde hūc sīs. L.S. Quid tibi vīs reddam?
EUC. Rogās?
635 L.S. Nīl equidem tibi abstulī. EUC. At illud quod tibi abstulerās cedo.
636 Ecquid agis? L.S. Quid agam? EUC. Auferre nōn potes. L.S. Quid vīs tibi?
637 EUC. Pōne. L.S. Id quidem pol tē datāre crēdō cōnsuētum, senex.
638 EUC. Pōne, hōc sīs, aufer cavillam, nōn ego nunc nūgās agō.

1. What has the slave of Lyconides heard? (617)
2. What warning does he address to the goddess? (618)
3. Who does he think the person is who hid the gold? (619)
4. What promise does he make to the goddess? (621–622) What does he promise himself? (623)
5. How did Euclio react to the cawing and digging of the raven? (626–627)
6. To what does Euclio compare the slave of Lyconides? (628) How is the comparison appropriate? (628–629)
7. How does the slave react to being caught? (631–632)
8. What is Euclio careful not to mention as he struggles with the slave? (633–636)
9. How does the slave make a bad joke out of Euclio's command? (637)

639 **ēloquere**: imperative (**quīn** adds force to the imperative and need not be translated).
641 ***em**, here you are! look at that! **eccās:** = **ecce eās**, here they are!
642 **larva, -ae** (*f*), evil spirit, demon.
    intemperiae, -ārum (*f pl*), intemperate state of mind.
    īnsānia, -ae (*f*), unsoundness of mind, madness.
643 **pendeō, pendēre** (2), **pependī**, to be suspended, hang.
644 **fatēre:** = **fatēris**.
645 **tuī:** "of yours."
646 **nīve**, or if . . . not.
    Agedum: = **age** + **-dum** (the particle **dum** adds emphasis).
    excutiō, excutere (3), **excussī, excussum**, to shake out.
    pallium, -ī (*n*), pallium, a rectangular piece of material worn mainly by men as an outer garment (considered as a characteristically Greek form of dress = the Greek himation).
647 ***arbitrātus, -ūs** (*m*), choice, judgment.
    nē: supply **metuō**, "I'm afraid you have (it). . . ."
    tunica, -ae (*f*), tunic, undergarment of the Romans (= the Greek chiton).
648 **quam benignē:** "how kindly (you allow me to examine you)."
649 **sȳcophantia, -ae** (*f*) (*Greek loan word*), craft, cunning, deceit.
650 **prōferō, prōferre** (*irreg.*), **prōtulī, prōlātum**, to bring forth, show, display.
651 **scrūtor, scrūtārī** (1), **scrūtātus sum**, to search for something hidden.
    mittō: "I stop" (doing something + infinitive).
    ā, interjection expressing any of a variety of feelings.
652 **expetō, expetere** (3), **expetīvī** or **expetiī, expetītum**, to seek, desire (to do something + infinitive).
653 **īnsāniō** (4), to be out of one's mind, be mad.
654 **penes** (+ *acc.*), in the possession of. Here following its accusative object, **mē**, and separated from it by other words.
655 **Manē:** imperative, "Wait."
656 **turbō** (1), to cause disorder or confusion.
    āmittō: here in the sense of **dīmittō**, to send or allow to go away. **hic:** "he."
657 **postrēmō**, finally, after all.
    perscrūtō: = **perscrūtor** (the verb occurs as both regular and deponent in Plautus; see lines 620, 651, and 653 for deponent forms).
659 **sociennus, -ī** (*m*), partner, associate.
    interstringō, interstringere (3), **interstrīnxī, interstrīctum**, to strangle, throttle.
660 **annōn:** = **an** + **nōn**, "or not." **sīs:** = **sī vīs**.

The figures on the left in this relief from Pompeii could be imagined to be Euclio and the slave of Lyconides.

54

639	L.S.	Quid ergō pōnam? Quīn tū ēloquere quidquid est suō nōmine.
640		Nōn hercle equidem quicquam sūmpsī nec tetigī. EUC. Ostende hūc
		manūs.
641	L.S.	*(stretching out his hands)* Em tibi, ostendī, eccās. EUC. Videō. Age os-
		tende etiam tertiam.
642	L.S.	Larvae hunc atque intemperiae īnsāniaeque agitant senem.
643		Facisne iniūriam mihi? EUC. Fateor, quia nōn pendēs, maximam.
644		Atque id quoque iam fīet, nisi fatēre. L.S. Quid fatear tibi?
645	EUC.	Quid abstulistī hinc? L.S. Dī mē perdant, sī ego tuī quicquam abstulī,
646		*(aside)* nīve adeō abstulisse vellem. EUC. Agedum, excutiendum
		pallium—
647	L.S.	*(interrupting and shaking his cloak)* Tuō arbitrātū. EUC. *(resuming)* Nē
		inter tunicās habeās. L.S. *(offering himself provocatively)* Temptā quā
		libet.
648	EUC.	Vāh, scelestus quam benignē, ut nē abstulisse intellegam!
649		Nōvī sȳcophantiās. Age rūrsus. Ostende hūc manum
650		dexteram. L.S. *(offering his right hand)* Em! EUC. Nunc laevam ostende.
		L.S. *(offering both hands)* Quīn equidem ambās prōferō.
651	EUC.	Iam scrūtārī mittō. Redde hūc. L.S. Quid reddam? EUC. Ā, nūgās agis,
652		certē habēs. L.S. Habeō ego? Quid habeō? EUC. Nōn dīcō, audīre expetis.
653		Id meum, quidquid habēs, redde. L.S. Īnsānīs: perscrūtātus es
654		tuō arbitrātū, neque tuī mē quicquam invēnistī penes.
		(A noise is heard from inside the temple.)
655	EUC.	Manē, manē. Quis illic est? Quis hīc intus alter erat tēcum simul?
656		periī hercle: ille nunc intus turbat, hunc sī āmittō, hic abierit.
657		Postrēmō hunc iam perscrūtāvī, hic nihil habet. *(letting the slave of*
		Lyconides go with a final blow) Abī quō libet.
658	L.S.	*(withdrawing)* Iuppiter tē dīque perdant. EUC. *(aside)* Haud male ēgit
		grātiās.
659		*(going toward the temple)* Ībō intrō atque illī sociennō tuō iam inter-
		stringam gulam.
660		*(to the slave of Lyconides)* Fugisne hinc ab oculīs? Abīsne hinc annōn?
		L.S. *(pretending to depart)* Abeō. EUC. *(departing into the temple)*
		Cavē sīs tē videam.

1. **What does Euclio begin to do to the slave in line 640?**
2. **Why does the slave think Euclio is insane?** (642)
3. **What does Euclio threaten to do to the slave if he does not admit the theft?** (643–644)
4. **What does the slave admit in the aside to himself in line 646?**
5. **Why do you think Euclio asks the slave to show his hands a second time?** (649–650)
6. **What feeling does Euclio reveal by repeating the command** *redde* **(651, 653) even after he has searched the slave thoroughly?**
7. **What is Euclio's dilemma in line 656?**
8. **For what does Euclio think he should have been thanked?** (658)
9. **What does Euclio determine to do now?** (659)
10. **What does Euclio order the slave of Lyconides to do?** (660)

661 **ēmorior, ēmorī** (3), **ēmortuus sum**, to perish, die completely.
   mālim: present subjunctive of **mālō**.
   lētum, -ī (*n*), death.
664 **sēcum**: = **cum sē**.
666 **tantisper**, in the meantime, meanwhile.
   concesserō: future perfect where we would expect a simple future.
668 **sublinō, sublinere** (3), **sublēvī, sublitum**, to smear beneath. **sublinere ōs alicui**, to fool, cheat, bamboozle someone (from a trick in which a sleeping person's face would be painted).
   ōs, ōris (*n*), mouth, face.
671 **illīc**: = **illī** (dative singular) + **-ce**.
672 **dīcam**: instead of **dōnem**, which would have been expected.
   edat: present subjunctive of **edō, ēsse** (*irrèg.*), **ēdī, ēsum**, to eat.
   tam . . . quam, as well . . . as.
   perdō, perdere, (here) to throw away, waste.
674 *****Silvānus, -ī** (*m*), a Roman god associated with forest and uncultivated land.
   āvius, -a, -um, without roads or paths, unfrequented, remote.
675 **salictum, -ī** (*n*), a group of willows (**salix, salicis**, *f*).
   oppleō, opplēre (2), **opplēvī, opplētum**, to fill completely.
677 **eugae**: = **euge** (*interjection expressing delight, pleasure, or surprise*) (*Greek loan word*), oh, good! fine!
678 **praecurrō, praecurrere** (3), **praecucurrī, praecursum**, to run in front, hurry on ahead.
   īnscendō, īnscendere (3), **īnscendī, īnscēnsum**, to climb up or into.
680 **sēsē**: object of **manēre**, "to wait for."
   iusserat: with a simple past meaning (cf. **dīxeram**, line 287).
681 **malam rem**: see line 483.
   lucrum, -ī (*n*), profit.

This comic actor could be reciting the slave of Lyconides' line Eugae, eugae, dī mē salvum et servātum volunt (677).

661	L.S.	*(alone)* Ēmortuum ego mē mālim lētō malō
662		quam nōn ego illī dem hodiē īnsidiās senī.
663		*(thoughtfully)* Nam hīc iam nōn audēbit aurum abstrūdere:
664		crēdō efferet iam sēcum et mūtābit locum.
665		*(The temple door creaks open.)* Attat, foris crepuit. *(Euclio reappears coddling the pot.)* Senex eccum aurum effert forās.
		(concealing himself at the door of Megadorus' house)
666		Tantisper hūc ego ad iānuam concesserō.
667	EUC.	Fidēī cēnsēbam maximam multō fidem
668		esse; ea sublēvit ōs mihi paenissimē:
669		nisi subvēnisset corvus, periissem miser.
670		Nimis hercle ego illum corvum ad mē veniat velim
671		quī indicium fēcit, ut ego illīc aliquid bonī
672		dīcam; nam quod edat tam dem quam perdam.
673		*(thinking hard)* Nunc hoc ubi abstrūdam cōgitō sōlum locum.
674		Silvānī lūcus extrā mūrum est āvius,
675		crēbrō salictō opplētus. Ibi sūmam locum.
676		Certum est, Silvānō potius crēdam quam Fidēī.
		(Euclio goes off stage to the left.)
677	L.S.	*(alone)* Eugae, eugae, dī mē salvum et servātum volunt.
678		Iam ego illūc praecurram atque īnscendam aliquam in arborem
679		indeque observābō aurum ubi abstrūdat senex.
680		Quamquam hīc manēre mē erus sēsē iusserāt;
681		certum est, malam rem potius quaeram cum lucrō.

The slave of Lyconides rushes off in the same direction Euclio had gone.
The stage is empty for a few moments.

1. **What is the slave of Lyconides determined to do?** (661–662)
2. **What does he think Euclio will do?** (663–664)
3. **How does Euclio feel about the goddess Fides now?** (667–668)
4. **What would Euclio like to do to thank the raven?** (670–672) **What is he not willing to do?** (672)
5. **Where does he decide to hide the gold now?** (673–676) **Where is this place located?** (674) **For what three reasons might it be safer than the temple of Fides?** (673–675)
6. **What does the slave of Lyconides decide to do?** (678–679)
7. **What had his master ordered him to do?** (680)
8. **How does he justify disobeying his master?** (681)

682 **iūxtā**, nearby, alike, equally. With **mēcum**.
683 **super** (+ *abl.*), about, concerning, respecting.
684 **resecrō** (1), to repeat a solemn appeal, to ask again.
686 **facta**: supply **esse**.
687 **impetrāssere**: archaic future infinitive of **impetrō** (1).
688 **sīquidem**, if it really is possible that.
689 **vīnolentus, -a, -um**, drunk with wine.
690 **adversum** (+ *acc.*), opposite to, facing.
   mentior, mentīrī (4), **mentītus sum**, to lie.
691 *****nūtrīx, nūtrīcis** (*f*), nurse.
   uterum, -ī (*n*) (= **uterus, -ī**, *m*), womb.
692 **Lūcīna, -ae** (*f*), the goddess who brings children into the world, usually identified
   with Juno, or in later times, with Diana.
   tuam fidem: supply **rogō** or **implōrō**.
693 **tibi**: dative of reference, "for you."
   potior, potius, having greater power, more effective, carrying more weight. Here,
   than mere words.
   parturiō, parturīre (4), **parturīvī**, to be on the point of giving birth, to be in labor.
694 **hāc**: supply **viā**, "this way." **nātus, -ī** (*m*), son. **mī**: vocative of **meus**.
698 *****opperior, opperīrī** (4), **oppertus sum**, to wait for.
699 **īrāscor, īrāscī** (3), **īrātus sum**, to be angry.
   iniūrius, -a, -um, unjust, unfair.
700 **dē capite meō**: i.e., "about my life"; an exaggeration.
   comitium, -ī (*n*), an elective or judicial assembly. Citizens could be tried on capital
   charges (**dē capite meō**) only before the **comitia**; Lyconides, of course, exaggerates
   the gravity of the deliberations taking place in Megadorus' house.

Lyconides and Eunomia

Eunomia and her son Lyconides (LYC.) enter from the right, deep in conversation.

682	**LYC.**	Dīxī tibi, māter, iūxtā mēcum rem tenēs,
683		super Eucliōnis fīliā. Nunc tē obsecrō
684		resecrōque, māter, quod dūdum obsecrāveram:
685		fac mentiōnem cum avunculō, māter mea.
686	**EUN.**	Scīs tū facta velle mē quae tū velīs,
687		et istuc confīdō ā frātre mē impetrāssere;
688		et causa iūsta est, sīquidem ita est ut praedicās,
689		tē eam compressisse vīnolentum virginem.
690	**LYC.**	Egone ut tē adversum mentiar, māter mea?

(Within Euclio's house, Phaedria, PH., cries out in pain of labor.)

691	**PH.**	Periī, mea nūtrīx. Obsecrō tē, uterum dolet.
692		Iūnō Lūcīna, tuam fidem! **LYC.** Em, māter mea,
693		tibi rem potiōrem videō: clāmat, parturit.
694	**EUN.**	Ī hāc intrō mēcum, nāte mī, ad frātrem meum,
695		ut istuc quod mē ōrās impetrātum ab eō auferam.

(Eunomia enters Megadorus' house.)

696	**LYC.**	Ī, iam sequor tē, māter. *(alone)* Sed servum meum
697		. . . . mīror ubi sit, quem ego mē iusseram
698		hīc opperīrī. Nunc ego mēcum cōgitō:
699		sī mihi dat operam, mē illī īrāscī iniūrium est.

(following his mother into Megadorus' house)

700		Ībō intrō, ubi dē capite meō sunt comitia.

1. **What has Lyconides just explained to his mother?** (682–683)
2. **What does he beg his mother to do now?** (683–685)
3. **How does Eunomia feel toward Lyconides?** (686)
4. **Does she think she will be successful in her appeal to Megadorus?** (687)
5. **What happens to prove that the story Lyconides has been telling his mother is true?** (691–693)
6. **With what purpose in mind does Eunomia enter Megadorus' house?** (694–695)
7. **What is Lyconides puzzled about?** (696–698)
8. **How does he give his slave the benefit of the doubt?** (698–699)
9. **How serious does Lyconides consider the matter to be that Eunomia has gone inside to discuss with Megadorus?** (700)

701 **pīx, pīcis** (*f*) (*Greek loan word*), a sphinx. In our passage the word is masculine and may refer to griffins. Legendary griffins were thought of as guarding gold in remote eastern regions (see the Greek historian Herodotus, III.116 and IV.13, 27).
    pīcīs: = **pīcēs**.
    *****dīvitiae, -ārum** (*f pl*), riches, wealth.
    aureus, -a, -um, golden.
    montīs: = **montēs**.
702 **istōs**: i.e., those commonly admired.
703 **mendīcābulum, -ī** (*n*), an instrument of a beggar's trade. **hominum mendīcābula**: "beggarly fellows."
704 **ille**: i.e., the renowned.
    rēx Philippus: see line 86. Plautus' audience would also think of Philip V of Macedon, defeated by the Romans at Cynoscephalae in 197 B.C.
    lepidus, -a, -um, charming, delightful. **lepidum diem**: exclamatory accusative.
705 **illō**: i.e., Euclio; ablative of comparison with **prior**.
    *****adveniō, advenīre** (4), **advēnī, adventum**, to arrive.
706 **collocō** (1), to put or set in a particular place.
707 **exspectō** (1), to wait for.
711 **dēclīnō** (1), to divert, turn away.
    paululum, a little.
714 **caecus, -a, -um**, blind.
715 **invēstīgō** (1), to search out, track down, find out.
    mī auxiliō: double dative with **sītis** (716).
716 *****obtestor, obtestārī** (1), **obtestātus sum**, to call upon as witness.
717 **vultus, -ūs** (*m*), expression, features, face.
718 **complūrēs, -ēs, -ia**, a fair number, quite a number, many. **complūrīs**: = **complūrēs**.
719 **vestītus, -ūs** (*m*), clothing, dress.
    crēta, -ae (*f*), chalk (used to whiten a toga). **vestītū et crētā**: *hendiadys* (two nouns used instead of a noun and an adjective) for **vestītū crētātō**, "with whitened garments." This may refer to politicians or political candidates, who regularly whitened their togas with chalk.
720 *****hem** (*interjection expressing surprise, concern, or unhappiness*), what's that? ah! alas!
721 **heu** (*followed by exclamatory accusative; pronounced as one syllable*), alas.
721a *****perditus, -a, -um**, ruined, lost, done for.
    ōrnātus, -a, -um, equipped, furnished. With **pessimē**, badly, "I'm in a sorry plight."
722 **gemitus, -ī (-ūs)** (*m*), groaning, moaning.
    maestitia, -ae (*f*), sadness, sorrow, grief.
722a **offerō, offerre** (*irreg.*), **obtulī, oblātum**, to put in a person's path.
724 **concustōdiō** (4), to watch over, guard, protect.
724a **sēdulō**, with care, diligently, attentively.
    dēfraudō (1), to defraud, cheat.
725 **genius, -ī** (*m*), the male spirit of a **gēns** existing in the head of the family and in the divine or spiritual part of each member of the family.
725a **laetificō** (1), to gladden, cheer, (passive) to be pleased, rejoice.

The moment Lyconides enters Megadorus' house, his slave reappears from off stage at the left, excited and happy, holding the pot of gold and celebrating his good fortune.

701 L.S.   Pīcīs dīvitiīs, quī aureōs montīs colunt,
702   ego sōlus superō. Nam istōs rēgēs cēterōs
703   memorāre nōlō, hominum mendīcābula:
704   ego sum ille rēx Philippus. Ō lepidum diem!
705   Nam ut dūdum hinc abiī, multō illō advēnī prior
706   multōque prius mē collocāvī in arborem
707   indeque exspectābam, aurum ubi abstrūdēbat senex.
708   Ubi ille abiit, ego mē deorsum dūcō dē arbore,
709   effodiō aulam aurī plēnam. Inde ex eō locō
710   videō recipere sē senem; ille mē nōn videt,
711   nam ego dēclīnāvī paululum mē extrā viam.

        (The slave of Lyconides sees Euclio arriving from the left.)

712   Attat, eccum ipsum. *(departing off stage to the right)* Ībō ut hoc
        condam domum.

    EUC. *(entering in despair and darting back and forth in rage and sorrow)*
713   Periī, interiī, occidī. Quō curram? Quō nōn curram? Tenē, tenē. Quem?
        Quis?   SONG
714   Nesciō, nīl videō, caecus eō atque equidem quō eam aut ubi sim aut
        quī sim
715   nequeō cum animō certum invēstīgāre. *(to the audience)* Obsecrō ego
        vōs, mī auxiliō,
716   ōrō, obtestor, sītis et hominem dēmōnstrētis, quis eam abstulerit.
717   Quid āis tū? Tibi crēdere certum est, nam esse bonum ex vultū
        cognōscō.
718   Quid est? Quid rīdētis? Nōvī omnīs, sciō fūrēs esse hīc complūrīs,
719   quī vestītū et crētā occultant sēsē atque sedent quasi sint frūgī.
720   Hem, nēmō habet hōrum? Occīdistī. Dīc igitur, quis habet? Nescīs?
721   *(to himself)* Heu mē miserum, miserē periī,
721a   male perditus, pessimē ōrnātus eō:
722   tantum gemitī et malī maestitiaeque
722a   hic diēs mī obtulit, famem et pauperiem.
723   Perditissimus ego sum omnium in terrā;
723a   nam quid mī opus est vītā, quī tantum aurī
724   perdidī, quod concustōdīvī
724a   sēdulō? Ego mē dēfraudāvī
725   animumque meum geniumque meum;
725a   nunc eō aliī laetificantur
726   meō malō et damnō. Patī nequeō.

1. **How does the slave of Lyconides see himself in comparison with the legendary griffins of the golden mountains and with legendary kings?** (701–702)
2. **With whom does he equate himself?** (704)
3. **What has the slave done since he last departed from the stage?** (705–711)
4. **Where does the slave of Lyconides go, and what does he intend to do?** (712)
5. **What is Euclio's opinion of the people he addresses in the audience?** (717–719)
6. **In what terms does Euclio express his grief?** (721–726)

727 **quīnam, quaenam, quodnam,** what . . . tell me?
maereō, maerēre (2), to be sad, mourn, grieve.
729 *****pariō, parere** (3), **peperī, partum,** to give birth.
incertus, -a, -um, uncertain.
731 **Ego sum miser:** "It's I—(and I'm) miserable."
Immō ego sum: "No, I'm (the one who's) miserable."
732 **maestitūdō, maestitūdinis** (*f*), sadness, sorrow, grief.
obtingō, obtingere (3), **obtigī,** to fall to one's lot, happen to.
*****es:** imperative of **esse.**
735 **dēmereō, dēmerēre** (2), **dēmeruī, dēmeritum,** to earn, deserve.
736 **ob** (+ *acc.*), on account of. **quam ob rem:** "for which reason," "why," "so that." Here
introducing two result clauses (**facerēs . . . īrēs**).
perditum īrēs: = **perderēs.**
737 **impulsor, impulsōris** (*m*), one who incites to action, an instigator.
illiciō, illicere (3), **illexī, illectum,** to entice, attract, lure.
738 *****peccō** (1), to make a mistake, be wrong, do wrong.
*****culpa, -ae** (*f*), blame.
commereor, commerērī (2), **commeritus sum,** to merit fully, deserve.
739 *****ignōscō, ignōscere** (3), **ignōvī, ignōtum** (+ *dat.*), to forgive.
741 **īnfectus, -a, -um,** not done, undone.
742 **nisi vellent, nōn fieret:** a past contrary to fact condition (here with imperfect sub-
junctives).
743 **nervus, -ī** (*m*), sinew, muscle, nerve, apparatus for securing the feet or necks of prisoners.
*****ēnecō** (1), to kill.
744 **tactiō est:** see note on line 423; "What business do you have touching my. . . ?"
745 **vitium, -ī** (*n*), fault. *****amor, amōris** (*m*), love.
746 **istācine:** = **istā** + **-ce** + **-ne** (a particle added for emphasis).
tē . . . ausum (esse): exclamatory infinitive, "that you have dared . . . !"
impudēns, impudentis, shameless, impudent, brazen.
748 **clārus, -a, -um,** bright. Note that **lūcī** is masculine here.
dēripiō, dēripere (3), **dēripuī, dēreptum,** to tear or pull off.
749 **postid:** = **posteā.**
prehendō, prehendere (3), **prehendī, prehēnsum,** to seize, catch.
*****ēbrius, -a, -um,** drunk.
751 **impūnē,** without punishment.

This relief with comic masks may suggest that characters often talked at cross purposes in Roman comedy, as Euclio and Lyconides do here in our play.

Lyconides appears from Megadorus' house, unseen by Euclio.

727 LYC. Quīnam homō hīc ante aedīs nostrās ēiulāns conqueritur maerēns?
728   Atque hic quidem Eucliō est, ut opīnor. Oppidō ego interiī: palam est rēs,
729   scit peperisse iam, ut ego opīnor, fīliam suam. Nunc mī incertum est
730   abeam an maneam an adeam an fugiam. *(pausing to consider his next move)* Quid agam? Edepol nesciō.
731 EUC. *(as he hears Lyconides speaking)* Quis homō hīc loquitur? LYC. Ego sum miser. EUC. Immō ego sum, et miserē perditus,   RECITATIVE
732   cui tanta mala maestitūdōque obtigit. LYC. *(moving forward to address Euclio)* Animō bonō es.
733 EUC. Quō, obsecrō, pactō esse possum? LYC. Quia istuc facinus quod tuum
734   sollicitat animum, id ego fēcī et fateor. EUC. Quid ego ex tē audiō?
735 LYC. Id quod vērum est. EUC. Quid ego dē tē dēmeruī, adulēscēns, malī,
736   quam ob rem ita facerēs mēque meōsque perditum īrēs līberōs?
737 LYC. Deus mihi impulsor fuit, is mē ad illam illexit. EUC. Quōmodō?
738 LYC. Fateor peccāvisse mē et mē culpam commeritum sciō;
739   id adeō tē ōrātum adveniō ut animō aequō ignōscās mihi.
740 EUC. Cūr id ausus es facere ut id quod nōn tuum esset tangerēs?
741 LYC. Quid vīs fierī? Factum est illud: fierī īnfectum nōn potest.
742   Deōs crēdō voluisse; nam nisi vellent, nōn fieret, sciō.
743 EUC. At ego deōs crēdō voluisse ut apud mē tē in nervō ēnecem.
744 LYC. Nē istuc dīxeris. EUC. Quid tibi ergō meam mē invītō tactiō est?
745 LYC. Quia vīnī vitiō atque amōris fēcī. EUC. Homō audācissime,
746   cum istācine tē ōrātiōne hūc ad mē adīre ausum, impudēns!
747   Nam sī istuc iūs est ut tū istuc excūsāre possīs,
748   lūcī clārō dēripiāmus aurum matrōnīs palam,
749   postid sī prehēnsī sīmus, excūsēmus ēbriōs
750   nōs fēcisse amōris causā. Nimis vīle est vīnum atque amor,
751   sī ēbriō atque amantī impūnē facere quod libeat licet.

1. **What does Lyconides think is the reason for Euclio's being so upset?** (727–729)
2. **What state of mind does this put Lyconides into?** (729–730)
3. **Both Lyconides and Euclio say they are** *miser.* (731) **What reason does each have?**
4. **What does Lyconides confess in lines 733–734?**
5. **To what does Euclio think Lyconides is confessing?** (734) **What is the misunderstanding that makes this scene so funny?**
6. **Where does Lyconides place the blame for his wrongdoing?** (737)
7. **Why has Lyconides come to Euclio now?** (739)
8. **To what extent can the questions and statements in lines 740–742 apply to both the violation of the girl and the theft of the gold?**
9. **To what forces does Lyconides attribute responsibility for his action?** (745)
10. **How does Euclio react to this excuse?** (745–746)
11. **What action does Euclio say people could commit with impunity if Lyconides' excuse were accepted as valid?** (747–750)

752 **supplicō** (1), to kneel down, pray or beg humbly.
   stultitia, -ae (*f*), folly, foolishness, silliness.
753 ***pūrigō** (**pūrgō**) (1), to clean, purge oneself of an offense, apologize.
754 **attingō, attingere** (3), **attigī, attactum**, to touch. With **attactam** supply **esse ā tē**.
755 **causificor, causificārī** (1), to allege a reason, put forward a pretext.
756 **potissimum**, especially, above all.
   mē: ablative.
757 **tē**: ablative.
   meam esse oportēre: Lyconides claims that Phaedria ought to be his according to
   the laws of Athens (see line 793 of the Latin text).
758 **quīn**, (here) indeed, in fact.
759 ***referō, referre** (*irreg.*), **rettulī, relātum**, to bring back.
760 **dīca, -ae** (*f*) (*Greek loan word*), a lawsuit, legal action. **dīcam scrībere** (*Latin translation of a Greek phrase*), to write an indictment, bring a charge against someone.
761 **Ita . . . ut** (762): for the construction, see the note on line 445, and see also line
   496.
763 **reposcō, reposcere** (3), to demand back.
   cōnfiteor, cōnfitērī (2), **cōnfessus sum**, to admit.
765 **pernegō** (1), to deny completely.
   istaec: = **ista** (fem. nom. sing.) + **-ce**.
767 **dīmidius, -a, -um**, half. **potius** (*adv.*), more gladly, rather.
768 **tametsī**, although.
769 **sānus, -a, -um**, sane.
770 **rescīscō, rescīscere** (3), **rescīvī** or **resciī, rescītum**, to get to know, try to find out
   about.
   attineō, attinēre (3), **attinuī, attentum**, to concern, affect (+ **ad** and accusative).
771 **magna**: supply **rēs**. **ōtiōsē**, at one's leisure. **ōtium, -ī** (*n*), leisure.
775 **indipīscō, indipīscere** (3), to acquire, receive.
   excipiō, excipere (3), **excēpī, exceptum**, to take in, shelter. **ita**, yes, right.
776 **fallis**: = **falsum dīcis**, lie. **mē**: ablative, "with me."

Actors with comic masks

752	LYC.	Quīn tibi ultrō supplicātum veniō ob stultitiam meam.
753	EUC.	Nōn mī hominēs placent quī quandō male fēcērunt pūrigant.
754		Tū illam sciēbās nōn tuam esse: nōn attactam oportuit.
755	LYC.	Ergō quia sum tangere ausus, haud causificor quīn eam
756		ego habeam potissimum. EUC. Tūne habeās mē invītō meam?
757	LYC.	Haud tē invītō postulō; sed meam esse oportēre arbitror.
758		Quīn tū iam inveniēs, inquam, meam illam esse oportēre, Eucliō.
759	EUC.	Nisi refers— LYC. *(interrupting)* Quid tibi ego referam?
	EUC.	Quod surripuistī meum,
760		iam quidem hercle tē ad praetōrem rapiam et tibi scrībam dīcam.
761	LYC.	Surripiō ego tuum? Unde? Aut quid id est? EUC. Ita tē amābit Iuppiter,
762		ut tū nescīs. LYC. Nisi quidem tū mihi quid quaerās dīxeris.
763	EUC.	Aulam aurī, inquam, tē reposcō, quam tū cōnfessus es mihi
764		tē abstulisse. LYC. Neque edepol ego dīxī neque fēcī. EUC. Negās?
765	LYC.	Pernegō immō. Nam neque ego aurum neque istaec aula quae sit
766		sciō nec nōvī. EUC. Illam, ex Silvānī lūcō quam abstulerās, cedo.
767		Ī, refer. Dīmidiam tēcum potius partem dīvidam.
768		Tametsī fūr mihi es, molestus nōn erō. Ī vērō, refer.
769	LYC.	Sānus tū nōn es quī fūrem mē vocēs. Ego tē, Eucliō,
770		dē aliā rē rescīvisse cēnsuī, quod ad mē attinet;
771		magna est quam ego tēcum ōtiōsē, sī ōtium est, cupiō loquī.
772	EUC.	Dīc bonā fidē: tū id aurum nōn surripuistī? LYC. Bonā.
773	EUC.	Neque eum scīs quī abstulerit? LYC. Istuc quoque bonā. EUC. Atque id sī sciēs
774		quī abstulerit, mihi indicābis? LYC. Faciam. EUC. Neque partem tibi
775		ab eō quī habet indipīscēs neque fūrem excipiēs? LYC. Ita.
776	EUC.	Id sī fallis? LYC. Tum mē faciat quod vult magnus Iuppiter!

1. What point does Lyconides make in his favor in line 752? Why does he use the word *ultrō?*

2. What kind of man does Euclio say he dislikes? (753)

3. Since the deed has been done, what does Lyconides think he should now be able to do? (755–756)

4. What does Lyconides say that Euclio will discover? (758)

5. How does Lyconides react when Euclio tells him in lines 759–760 to return what he has stolen? (761–762)

6. How does Lyconides respond to Euclio's statement that he has confessed to stealing the pot of gold? (764)

7. What deal is Euclio willing to make? (767)

8. How does Lyconides try to change the subject to his love for Phaedria? (769–771)

9. What five questions does Lyconides have to answer before Euclio will believe that he did not steal the pot of gold? (772–776) What seems finally to convince him? (776)

777 **Satis habeō**: = **Sufficit**, "That's sufficient."
778 **nātus**: perfect participle of **nāscor**.
781 **eccillam**: "There she is!"
783 ***repudium, -ī** (*n*), repudiation or rejection of a prospective wife or husband, breaking
    of an engagement.
784 **exōrnō** (1), to equip, prepare.
785 **quantum est**: "as many as there are."
    perdant: subjunctive in a wish introduced by **ut**.
786 **īnfēlīx, īnfēlīcis**, unlucky, unfortunate, unhappy.
788 **fēlīciter**, with good fortune, fortunately, luckily.
    inquitō: future imperative.
790 **quī homō**: = **homō quī**.
    admittō, admittere (3), **admīsī, admissum**, to admit, incur (guilt, disgrace).
    nūllus: = **nōn**.
    parvī pretī: genitive of description.
791 **pudeō, pudēre** (2), **puduī, puditum**, to feel shame, be ashamed.
    pūrgō: = **pūrigō**.
792 **ergā** (+ *acc.*), to, toward.
    imprūdēns, imprūdentis, lacking in judgment or discretion, foolish, incautious.
795 **impulsus, -ūs** (*m*), thrust, prompting, impulse.
    adulēscentia, -ae (*f*), youth.
796 **ēiulō** (1), to exclaim **ei** (a shriek, wail).
799 **remittō, remittere** (3), **remīsī, remissum**, to send back.
800 ***exquīrō, exquīrere** (3), **exquīsīvī, exquīsītum**, to ask about, inquire into.
    -ne, whether.
801 **agglūtinō** (1), to stick, glue, attach.

Relief showing a comic actor and a boy holding a mask.

777	EUC.	Satis habeō. Age nunc loquere quid vīs. LYC. Sī mē nōvistī minus,
778		genere quō sim nātus: hic mihi est Megadōrus avunculus,
779		meus fuit pater Antimachus, ego vocor Lycōnidēs,
780		māter est Eunomia. EUC. Nōvī genus. Nunc quid vīs? Id volō
781		nōscere. LYC. Fīliam ex tē tū habēs. EUC. Immō eccillam domī.
782	LYC.	Eam tū dēspondistī, opīnor, meō avunculō. EUC. Omnem rem tenēs.
783	LYC.	Is mē nunc renūntiāre repudium iussit tibi.
784	EUC.	(furious) Repudium rēbus parātīs, exōrnātīs nūptiīs?
785		Ut illum dī immortālēs omnēs deaeque quantum est perdant,
786		quem propter hodiē aurī tantum perdidī īnfēlīx, miser.
787	LYC.	Bonō animō es, bene dīc. Nunc quae rēs tibi et nātae tuae
788		bene fēlīciterque vertat—ita dī faciant, inquitō.
789	EUC.	Ita dī faciant. LYC. Et mihi ita dī faciant. Audī nunciam.
790		Quī homō culpam admīsit in sē, nūllus est tam parvī pretī
791		quīn pudeat, quīn pūrget sēsē. Nunc tē obtestor, Eucliō,
792		ut sī quid ego ergā tē imprūdēns peccāvī aut nātam tuam,
793		ut mī ignōscās eamque uxōrem mihi dēs, ut lēgēs iubent.
794		Ego mē iniūriam fēcisse fīliae fateor tuae
795		Cereris vigiliīs per vīnum atque impulsū adulēscentiae.
796	EUC.	Ei mihi, quod ego facinus ex tē audiō? LYC. Cūr ēiulās,
797		quem ego avum fēcī iam ut essēs fīliae nūptiīs?
798		Nam tua nāta peperit, decimō mēnse post: numerum cape;
799		eā rē repudium remīsit avunculus causā meā.
800		Ī intrō, exquīre sitne ita ut ego praedicō. EUC. Periī oppidō,
801		ita mihi ad malum malae rēs plūrimae sē agglūtinant.
802		Ībō intrō, ut quid huius vērum sit sciam. LYC. (to Euclio as he enters his house) Iam tē sequor.

1. How does Lyconides introduce himself? (777–780)
2. What news does Lyconides bring from his uncle Megadorus? (783)
3. How does Euclio react to this news? (784–786)
4. Whom does Euclio blame for the fact that he has lost his gold? (785–786)
5. How does Lyconides try to cheer Euclio up? (787)
6. For what does Lyconides make Euclio pray to the gods? (787–789)
7. What, according to Lyconides, do people do who have done wrong? (790–791)
8. What two things does Lyconides ask of Euclio? (793)
9. What does Lyconides confess that he did? (794–795)
10. What reason does Lyconides give why Euclio should be happy instead of miserable? (797–798)
11. Why, according to Lyconides, did Megadorus break his engagement? (799)
12. Is Euclio cheered by the news that Lyconides has brought? (800–801)
13. With what intention does Euclio enter the house? (802)

803 **propemodum**, virtually, just about.
    vadum, -ī (*n*), a shallow place in water (here of shallow water as a place of safety for a swimmer). **in vadō salūtis**: "in the haven of safety."
805 **paulīsper**, briefly.
806 **subsequor, subsequī** (3), **subsecūtus sum**, to follow closely upon.
807 **pedisequa, -ae** (*f*), a female attendant, waiting-woman.
808 **dōnō** (1), to present, endow, reward with. **gaudium, -ī** (*n*), joy.
809 ***quadrilībris, -is, -e**, containing four pounds weight (**lībra, -ae**, *f*, a measure of weight containing twelve Roman ounces, a pound). **dīs, dītis**, wealthy, rich.
810 **quis . . . quisquam**: redundant, "what man at all."
    Athēnae, -ārum (*f pl*), Athens.
    magis: with **propitiī**.
    propitius, -a, -um, favorably inclined, propitious, well disposed.
811 **enim**, (here) indeed.
813 **contollō, contollere** (3), to bring up. ***gradum contollere**, to step up (to meet a person).
817 **igitur**, then.
    ***ēmittō, ēmittere** (3), **ēmīsī, ēmissum**, to send out, release, free. ***manū ēmittere**, to discharge a slave from one's power.
818 **clāmitō** (1), to shout repeatedly.
819 **faba, -ae** (*f*), a bean. It is not known what the boys in this proverbial saying found (perhaps a worm, i.e., a trifle).
    dēlūdō, dēlūdere (3), **dēlūsī, dēlūsum**, to make a game of, deceive, dupe.
821 **nimius, -a, -um**, excessive, extraordinary.
    ubinam: an emphatic **ubi**.
823 **arca, -ae** (*f*), chest (for money).

Could this be the slave of Lyconides defying his master? (Compare line 831)

LYC. *(alone, in relief and satisfaction)*

803 Haec propemodum iam esse in vadō salūtis rēs vidētur.
804 Nunc servum esse ubi dīcam meum . . . . nōn reperiō:
805 nisi etiam hic opperiar tamen paulīsper; posteā intrō
806 hunc subsequar. Nunc interim spatium eī dabō exquīrendī
807 meum factum ex nātae pedisequā nūtrīce anū: ea rem nōvit.

Lyconides lingers outside Euclio's house. His slave, who has secreted the pot of gold at home, now returns from the right, still filled with euphoria. He does not see Lyconides.

808 L.S. Dī immortālēs, quibus et quantīs mē dōnātis gaudiīs!
809 Quadrilībrem aulam aurō onustam habeō. Quis mē est dītior?
810 Quis mē Athēnīs nunc magis quisquam est homō cui dī sint propitiī?
811 LYC. *(hearing someone speaking)* Certō enim ego vōcem hīc loquentis modo
mī audīre vīsus sum. L.S. *(catching sight of his master)* Hem,
812 erumne ego aspiciō meum? LYC. *(seeing his slave)* Videōne ego hunc
servum meum?
813 L.S. *(to himself)* Ipse est. LYC. *(to himself)* Haud alius est. L.S. *(to himself, as
he goes up to his master)* Congrediar. LYC. *(to himself, as he approaches his slave)* Contollam gradum.
814-815 Crēdō ego illum, ut iussī, ipsam anum adiisse, huius nūtrīcem virginis.
L.S. *(still to himself, as he approaches his master)*
816 Quīn ego illī mē invēnisse dīcō hanc praedam atque ēloquor?
817 Igitur ōrābō ut manū mē ēmittat. *(approaching closer)* Ībō atque
ēloquar.
818 *(to Lyconides)* Repperī— LYC. *(interrupting)* Quid repperistī? L.S. Nōn
quod puerī clāmitant
819 in fabā sē repperisse. LYC. Iamne autem, ut solēs? Dēlūdis.
L.S. *(to Lyconides, who turns to leave in annoyance)*
820 Ere, manē, ēloquar iam, auscultā. LYC. *(remaining)* Age ergō loquere.
L.S. Repperī hodiē,
821 ere, dīvitiās nimiās. LYC. Ubinam? L.S. Quadrilībrem, inquam, aulam
aurī plēnam.
822 LYC. Quod ego facinus audiō ex tē? L.S. *(teasingly)* Eucliōnī huic senī
surripuī.
823 LYC. *(now attentive and interested)* Ubi id est aurum? L.S. In arcā apud mē.
(pleading) Nunc volō mē ēmittī manū.

1. **How does Lyconides assess the situation?** (803) **Whom is he looking for?** (804)
2. **Why does Lyconides wait outside instead of following Euclio immediately into the house?** (805–807)
3. **For what is Lyconides' slave thanking the gods?** (808–810)
4. **By what stages do Lyconides and his slave approach one another?** (811–813)
5. **What does Lyconides think that his slave has been doing?** (814–815)
6. **What does Lyconides' slave decide to ask his master?** (817)
7. **Does the slave tell his master about the gold directly?** (818–822) **How is his way of revealing what he has done in keeping with his character?** (819)
8. **Do you think Lyconides' response in line 822 is what his slave expected?**
9. **What does the slave persist in asking for?** (823)

825 **scelus, sceleris** (*n*), crime, villainy.
   cumulātus, -a, -um, heaped, abounding in (+ genitive).
826 **abī** (*a colloquial expression*), away with you! enough!
827 **lepidē**, facetiously, merely for fun, in sport.
   ēripiō, ēripere (3), **ēripuī, ereptum**, to seize, snatch from.
   apparō (1), to prepare, plan to.
828 **probāre**, (here) to win approval for. "You can't get away with your joking."
830 **fassus es**: from **fateor**.
   arca, -ae (*f*), chest.
   garriō, garrīre (4), **garrīvī**, to chatter, talk nonsense.
831 **quōmodo**: i.e., "how (I will handle you)."
   vel: reinforces the imperative and need not be translated.

I **uxōrius, -a, -um**, of or belonging to a wife.
II **admordeō, admordēre** (2), **admemordī, admorsum**, to bite at, gnaw.
III **dēnī, -ae, -a**, ten each, ten together.
   scrobis, scrobis (*m/f*), a hole dug in the ground (usually for planting trees).
IV **diū**, (here) by day.
V **holus, holeris** (*n*), vegetables.   **hallec, hallecis** (*n*), a fish sauce.
   addō, addere (3), **addidī, additum**, to place along with.

Plautus' play ended with Euclio recovering his gold and bestowing his daughter upon Lyconides. This relief shows the dextrārum iunctiō of a Roman marriage ceremony.

70

824	LYC.	*(enraged)* Egone tē ēmittam manū,
825		scelerum cumulātissime?
826	L.S.	*(laughing)* Abī, ere, sciō quam rem gerās.
827		Lepidē hercle animum tuum temptāvī. Iam ut ēriperēs apparābās.
828		Quid facerēs, sī repperissem? LYC. *(sternly)* Nōn potes probāre nūgās.
829		Ī, redde aurum. L.S. Reddam ego aurum? LYC. Redde, inquam, ut huic reddātur. L.S. Unde?
830	LYC.	Quod modo fassus es esse in arcā. L.S. Soleō hercle ego garrīre nūgās.
831		Ita loquor. LYC. *(catching hold of his slave)* At scīsne quōmodo? L.S. Vel hercle ēnecā, numquam hinc ferēs ā mē.

1. **How does Lyconides react to his slave's plea for freedom?** (824–825)
2. **How does the slave change his tune when he realizes his master is angry with him?** (826–827)
3. **With what does he charge Lyconides?** (827)
4. **What does he pretend had never happened?** (828)
5. **Why does Lyconides want the money returned?** (829)
6. **Is the slave willing to return it?** (829–831)

The remainder of the play has been lost except for a few fragments printed below. Some idea of how the play ended can be conjectured from these fragments and the summaries of the plot (**argūmenta**) written later in antiquity which precede the text of the play in the manuscripts.

prō illīs crocōtīs, strophiīs, sūmptū uxōriō	I
ut admemordit hominem	II
EUC. Ego effodiēbam in diē dēnōs scrobīs.	III
EUC. Nec noctū nec diū quiētus umquam eram; nunc dormiam.	IV
L.S. Quī mī holera crūda pōnunt, hallec addant.	V

Fragment IV may refer to Euclio's anxiety over the pot of gold and his relief when he finally gives it to Lyconides as a dowry to accompany his daughter. The first of the ancient plot summaries (**argūmenta**) says that Euclio unexpectedly recovers his pot of gold and then happily bestows his daughter upon Lyconides (**īnspērātō invenit / laetusque nātam collocat Lycōnidī**). The second plot summary says that Lyconides tells Euclio that his slave has stolen Euclio's pot of gold (**illic Eucliōnī rem refert**) and that Euclio gives Lyconides the gold, a wife, and a son (**ab eō dōnātur aurō, uxōre et fīliō**). There is no suggestion of what happens to Lyconides' slave.

For a full discussion of the ending of the play, see Edwin L. Minar, Jr., "The Lost Ending of Plautus' *Aulularia*," *The Classical Journal* 42 (1946–1947), pp. 271–275. Endings are supplied for the play in two editions published in Italy in A.D. 1500. See the appendices in R. J. Thomas' edition of the play (*T. Macci Plauti Aulularia*, Oxford, 1913).

Deeply impressed by their Greek literary forerunners, the Romans borrowed extensively from Greek works and their debt gave added cachet to their own efforts. While Plautus does not reveal the sources of his *Aulularia*, we can see some points of similarity in Menander's *Dyskolos (The Grouch)*, which won first prize when it was originally produced at a winter festival in Athens in 316 B.C. The play, discovered some twenty-five years ago in a mid third century A.D. papyrus from Egypt, deals with a bad-tempered, misanthropic, miserly man, Knemon, divorced from his wife and living with his daughter, Myrrhine, in the country outside Athens near a shrine of the Nymphs. The prologue is spoken by the god Pan, who enters from the cave of the Nymphs, and it bears a number of resemblances to that spoken by Plautus' Lar (*Aulularia* 1–39). The translation is that of Carroll Moulton.

PAN

Our scene's the countryside, in Attica,
where farmers till the rocks for bread. This place
is Phyle. The Nymphs are famous here:
their sacred cave is right behind me.
5   On my right, the farm is owned by Knemon,
a man self-exiled from the human race:
an utter grouch and not gregarious.
That understates the case! He's over sixty
and refuses to enjoy a chat with anyone.
10   Because we're neighbors, he consents to greet me,
though this is an exception to his rule.
I'm sure he's promptly sorry he's been civil.
All the same, despite this temperament,
he got married to a widow. Her first husband
15   had just died and left behind a son:
the child was very young then.
The marriage was more like suing for divorce,
with sessions held all day and half the night.
Knemon nagged and was unhappy. When a little girl
20   was born, things went from bad to worse. When nothing else
could change her bitter, dreary way of life,
his wife renounced the grouch, sought out her son
again, and lived with him. He owns a little
piece of land here, barely big enough
25   to feed himself, his mother, and a single
servant, faithful to the family.
The lad's turned out a fine young man,
who boasts a fund of sense beyond his years:
maturity comes easily when life goes hard.

30 Old Knemon grouches on, his solitude
    intact but for his daughter and a servant hag.
    He carries logs, and digs, and sweats,
    and hates the world in order: starting here
    with wife and neighbors, and going on for miles
35 down the road. A lonely childhood, though,
    has kept his daughter innocent: piously
    she tends this shrine. Her care of us inclines
    my Nymphs and me to keep a special watch
    on her. So, when a young man from the town,
40 whose father is extremely rich and owns
    some large estates, came out to hunt here with
    a friend, he chanced upon our neighborhood
    and fell in love with Knemon's daughter. (You
    might say a god had had a hand in it.)
45 These are the highlights: if you wish to see
    the details (as I hope you do), you will.

As the play progresses, Knemon, who wants to be left alone, complains
bitterly about people coming to worship and sacrifice at the nearby cave of
the Nymphs. He shouts at Geta, slave of the family of Sostratos (the young
man in love with Knemon's daughter), who is preparing a sacrifice and
wishes to borrow a kettle. Knemon's nature and reactions recall Euclio's
handling of the cooks sent by Megadorus (*Aulularia* 388–448):

GETA *(to the servants inside the shrine of the Nymphs)*
You say you left the stewing pot behind?
You must all be hung over. Now what do we do?
[moves toward KNEMON's house]
I guess I'll have to bother the god's neighbors.
[knocks at KNEMON's door]
Hey, there, inside, boy! . . .
What's going on here? Slaves! There's not a soul
465 inside. *[listens at the door]* Ah, now there's someone coming out.
[enter KNEMON, furious]

KNEMON
You thrice accursed being, why's your hand
upon my door? Speak up!

GETA *(stepping back)*
Don't bite!

KNEMON
            I'll bite
and eat you too, God damn it!

GETA
            Good lord, calm down!

KNEMON
You wretch, have you and I got business with
each other?

GETA

470   Oh, no, no business. Look—I haven't
brought a witness: I'm not collecting debts.
I've come to ask you for a stewing pot.

KNEMON (incredulous)

A stewing pot?

GETA

A pot.

KNEMON

                You ought to get a whipping!
You think I've got an ox to sacrifice,
the way you people do?

GETA (aside)

475   You probably
don't have a snail. [hastily] Good-bye, good sir. The girls
inside the shrine requested me to knock
upon your door and ask. I did. You have no pots.
I'll tell them that when I get back.
        [muttering, as he leaves] Gods above!

480 The old man bites just like a snake! [Exit]

KNEMON

Wild animals, they are! They come right up
and knock as if you were a friend. [turns toward the shrine] If I
catch any man come to my door, and don't
make an example out of him, then

485 count me as a nobody. I don't
know how this guy got off so well just now. [Exit]

Later in the play Knemon falls into the well while trying to retrieve his
pickax, and he is rescued by his stepson Gorgias with aid from Sostratos, the
young man who wants to marry Knemon's daughter. This experience teaches
Knemon several lessons and produces a change in his thinking that will
eventually permit two marriages to take place at the end of the play. Compare the change that must have taken place in Euclio in the now lost conclusion of the *Aulularia*—a change that may have been precipitated by Euclio's
loss of his pot of gold just as the change in Knemon is precipitated by his fall
down the well.

KNEMON

It seems we only learn our lessons when
700 we suffer some bad accident.
                . . . Not one of you
could make me change my mind. You'll have to let me have
my way. I think I've made just one mistake. That was
to feel that I alone was self-sufficient and
715 would need no one. Now that I see how death can be
so swift and sudden, I know that I was wrong in this.
A man needs someone standing by to help him out.

74

I hadn't admitted that before, because I thought
that every man around cared only for his own
720 profit. By God, I thought there wasn't one of them
who was concerned for other men. That was what blinded me.
One man has just now proved the opposite:
Gorgias, who's done a deed that's worthy of
the finest gentleman. I never let him near
725 my door, or gave him help in anything.
or greeted or conversed with him, and still he saved me.
Another man might well have said: "You don't allow
me in—well, I won't come. You've never helped us out—
I won't help you." [catches sight of GORGIAS, who has
now returned, and looks embarrassed]
What's the matter, boy? If I
730 should die—I think that's likely, seeing as how I feel—
or whether I live, I'm making you my legal son,
and heir to what I own. It's yours. And take the girl:
she's in your care. Find her a man. For even if
I live, I won't be able to. Not a single one
735 will ever please me. If I survive, though, let
me live the way I want. Do all else as you wish.
Thank God, you're sensible. You're just the man to be
your sister's guardian. Give half of my estate
as dowry for her; the rest can feed me and your mother.

* * *

Molière adapted the character of Euclio for his comedy *L'Avare* (*The Miser*),
first produced in Paris in 1668 with the playwright himself appearing as
Harpagon, the miser. This name may have been suggested by the Latin verb
harpagō "to steal, carry off," used in the *Aulularia* (201). The widower Harpagon has a son Cléante, in love with Mariane, and a daughter Elise, in love
with Valère, the brother of Mariane. Obsessed with money, he has buried a
cash box containing 10,000 crowns, about which he worries throughout the
play. This treasure is stolen by La Flèche, Cléante's valet, but Valère, who is
acting as Harpagon's steward, is accused of the theft and brought before a
magistrate. The plot is complicated by the two sets of lovers, by Harpagon's
plan to marry Mariane, unaware of his son's interest in her, and by Harpagon's wish to betroth his daughter Elise to Anselme, who turns out to be the
long-lost father of Mariane and Valère. All ends happily for the lovers when
Cléante agrees to return his father's treasure if he is allowed to marry Mariane and when Anselme agrees to pay all the wedding expenses.

In Act I, Scene 3, Harpagon upbraids Cléante's valet, La Flèche, just as
Euclio scolds Staphyla (*Aulularia* 40–104), betrays his fear about his money
(cf. *Aulularia* 105–119 and elsewhere), and, accusing La Flèche of robbery,
searches him as Euclio searches Lyconides' slave (*Aulularia* 628–654). The
translation is that of Wallace Fowlie.

LA FLÈCHE. My master—your son—told me to wait for him.
HARPAGON. Wait for him in the street, and don't stay in this house,
erect like a watchman, and with an eye on everything that happens and
picking up what you can. I don't want a spy in my house, a sneak look-

ing at everything I do with his accursed eyes, devouring what I possess and rummaging everywhere to see if there's anything he can steal.

LA FLÈCHE. How the devil do you think anyone can steal from you? It can't be done, because you lock up everything and stand guard day and night.

HARPAGON. I'll lock up whatever I want to and stand guard whenever I want to. *(aside)* They're all a pack of prying rascals watching everything that is done. I only fear he has some suspicion about my money. *(aloud)* Aren't you the kind of man who would spread the rumor that I have money hidden in my house?

LA FLÈCHE. Do you have money hidden away?

HARPAGON. No, you scoundrel, I didn't say that. *(aside)* He infuriates me. *(aloud)* I only wondered if maliciously you wouldn't spread the rumor that I have hidden some away. . . . Once more, get out of here!

LA FLÈCHE. All right! I'm leaving.

HARPAGON. Stop! Are you taking anything with you?

LA FLÈCHE. What could I be taking?

HARPAGON. Let me see. Show me your hands.

LA FLÈCHE. Look at them.

HARPAGON. Now the others.

LA FLÈCHE. The others?

HARPAGON. Yes.

LA FLÈCHE. Here you are.

HARPAGON. *(points to LA FLÈCHE's breeches)* Did you put anything here?

LA FLÈCHE. Why don't you look?

HARPAGON. *(feels the bottom of the breeches)* These wide breeches are just right for hiding things that are stolen. I wish they'd hang the man who made them.

LA FLÈCHE. *(aside)* A man like him deserves what he expects. I wish I could have the pleasure of robbing him.

HARPAGON. Eh?

LA FLÈCHE. What?

HARPAGON. What did you say about robbing?

LA FLÈCHE. I said that you're poking about everywhere to see if I robbed you.

HARPAGON. That's what I mean to do *(He feels LA FLÈCHE's pockets.)* . . .

LA FLÈCHE. *(shows one of the pockets of his jerkin)* Here's one more pocket. Will that please you?

HARPAGON. All right! Give it over without my searching you.

LA FLÈCHE. Give over what?

HARPAGON. What you took from me.

LA FLÈCHE. I took nothing from you.

HARPAGON. Are you sure?

LA FLÈCHE. I am sure.

HARPAGON. Off with you, then. And the devil take you!

LA FLÈCHE. *(aside)* It's a fine way to be sent off.

In contrast to Megadorus' tirade against wives with large dowries (*Aulularia* 475–535), Frosine, a professional matchmaker, describes the economical habits of the intended bride, Mariane, who will have a "dowry" of 12,000 francs (Act II, Scene 5):

FROSINE. Why, this girl will bring you twelve thousand francs a year.

HARPAGON. Twelve thousand francs a year!

FROSINE. Yes. First of all, she has been brought up on a very spare diet. She is a girl accustomed to live on salad, milk, cheese, and apples. Therefore she won't need a rich menu: no fine consommes, no eternal barley dishes, none of the delicacies another woman would want. This is no small consideration. Every year it might go up to three thousand francs at least. Moreover, her tastes are very simple. She doesn't like elaborate dresses or expensive jewels, or sumptuous furniture which women of her age are so crazy about. And this means a saving of more than four thousand francs a year. In addition to this, she has a great distaste for gambling, which is unusual for women today. I know one in our neighborhood who this year lost twenty thousand francs at cards (let's just take a fourth of that), plus four thousand francs in dresses and jewels makes nine thousand, and another three thousand for food,—that gives you twelve thousand francs a year, doesn't it?. . .

HARPAGON. It's a mockery to try to build up her dowry out of expenses she won't incur. I won't get a receipt for what I don't receive. I have to have something I can put my hands on.

In Act IV, Scene 7, Harpagon hysterically laments the theft of his money in a manner reminiscent of Euclio (*Aulularia* 713–726):

HARPAGON. *(shouts "stop, thief" and comes in hatless)* Thieves! murderers! Justice, merciful heaven! They've killed me, they've cut my throat, they've stolen my money. Who can it be? What became of him? Where is he? Where is he hiding? How can I find him? Where should I run to? Where shouldn't I run to? Is he over there? Is he here? Who is it? Stop. Give me back my money, you rascal . . . *(catches his own arm)* Oh! it's me. I'm out of my mind. I don't know where I am, or who I am, or what I'm doing. Oh! my poor money, my darling money! They've taken you away. And because you're not here, I've lost my strength, my consolation, my happiness. All is over for me. I can't go on. I'm dying. I'm dead and buried. Is there no one who will bring me back to life, and give me back my beloved money, or tell me who took it. What? What did you say? No one's there. Whoever did the deed knew exactly the right time. Just at the time I was talking to my villain of a son. I must go. I will demand justice and have everyone in the house questioned: servants, valets, my son, my daughter, myself too. Everyone will be there. I suspect everyone I look at. They all look like thieves. What are they talking about over there? About the fellow who robbed me? What is that noise up there? Please, if you know anything about my thief, please tell me. You aren't hiding him, are you? They are all looking at me. And beginning to laugh. You will see that they are involved in this robbery, beyond any doubt. Come here quickly: police, provosts, judges, racks, gallows and hangmen. I want them all to be hanged. And if I don't get my money back, I'll hang myself afterwards.

Whereas Euclio threatens to charge Lyconides with theft before a magistrate (*Aulularia* 759–760), Harpagon actually summons Valère, his steward (in love with his daughter Elise) before a magistrate on a charge made by Master Jacques, Harpagon's cook and coachman, that he stole Harpagon's money. The ensuing scene contains the same misunderstanding of what has been stolen as develops in the *Aulularia*: the confusion of **aula** and **filia** in the Latin play is repeated in confusion over *cassette* (cash box) and *fille* (daughter) in the French. Like Euclio (*Aulularia* 800–801), Harpagon is more distressed than pleased by the revelation of the true state of affairs (Act V, Scene 3):

HARPAGON. Come here! Come and confess the darkest, the foulest crime ever committed.

VALÈRE. What do you mean, sir?

HARPAGON. You scoundrel! Don't you blush for your crime?

VALÈRE. What crime are you talking about?

HARPAGON. What crime am I talking about? You wretch, as if you didn't know what I am talking about! There's no use in trying to hide it. You have been found out and I have just learned the whole story. . . .

VALÈRE. Sir, since you have been told everything, I won't attempt any evasions, or try to deny it. . . . I intended to speak to you about this, and I was simply waiting for a good opportunity. But since it has turned out this way, I beg you not to be angry and to listen to what I have to say.

HARPAGON. What can you say for yourself, you rascal of a thief?

VALÈRE. Sir, I do not deserve such a name. It is true that I have committed an offense against you, but after all, my fault is pardonable.

HARPAGON. Pardonable, you say! Such a dastardly trick? Such a stab-in-the-back?. . . But, tell me, what led you to do such a thing?

VALÈRE. Are you really asking this?

HARPAGON. Yes, I am asking you.

VALÈRE. The god of Love who pardons a man for all he makes you do.

HARPAGON. Love?

VALÈRE. Yes.

HARPAGON. A fine love, on my word. Love for my gold pieces.

VALÈRE. No, sir, I am not tempted by your wealth. That is not what dazzled me. I insist that I do not covet your wealth, provided you let me keep the treasure I already have.

HARPAGON. I will not. Not by all the demons in hell. I will not let you keep it. You are impudent in wanting to keep what you have stolen. . . . But I want restoration. You must confess where the hiding place is.

VALÈRE. Why, there is no hiding place. We never left your house.

HARPAGON. *(aside)* O my beloved money box! *(to VALÈRE)* Did not leave the house, you say?

VALÈRE. No, sir.

HARPAGON. Now, tell me. Did you touch . . . ?

VALÈRE. Never! You are wronging both of us. I am deeply in love, but honorably . . .

HARPAGON. *(aside)* In love with my money box!

VALÈRE. I would rather die than manifest any thought offensive to one so kind and modest.

HARPAGON. *(aside)* My money box is modest!

VALÈRE. My desire was limited to the pleasure of looking at her, and nothing criminal ever debased the passion her beauty inspired in me.

HARPAGON. *(aside)* The beauty of my money box! You might think he is a lover talking about a mistress.

VALÈRE. Dame Claude knows the truth about this matter, and she will testify that . . .

HARPAGON. So, my servant is an accomplice too!

VALÈRE. Yes, sir. She was a witness to our engagement, and when she

learned the honorable intentions of my love, she helped persuade your
daughter to give me her promise and accept mine. . . .

HARPAGON. Why are you mixing up my daughter in all this?

VALÈRE. I am saying, sir, that I had the greatest difficulty in making her
modesty consent to my love.

HARPAGON. Whose modesty?

VALÈRE. Your daughter's. Not until yesterday did she and I sign a promise of marriage.

HARPAGON. Did my daughter sign a marriage promise?

VALÈRE. Yes, sir, and I signed one too.

HARPAGON. Oh Heavens! Another disaster!

In contrast to Menander's *Dyskolos* and Plautus' *Aulularia*, in which the
misanthrope and miser respectively change their ways of thinking and help
bring about the happy endings of those plays, Harpagon retains his pathologi-
cal fixation on his money box to the very end of the play and refuses to
contribute anything to the marriages of his children (Act V, Scene 6):

CLÉANTE. Stop being worried, father, and don't accuse anyone. I have
news about your money, and I have come to tell you that if you consent
to let me marry Mariane, your money will be returned to you.

HARPAGON. Where is it?

CLÉANTE. There is no need for worry. It is in a safe place and I am responsible. It is up to you to tell me what you decide. The choice is
yours: either to give me Mariane or lose your money box.

HARPAGON. Has anything been taken from it?

CLÉANTE. No, nothing. Is it your intention to allow this marriage, and
add your consent to her mother's who leaves Mariane free to choose
between us.

MARIANE. (*to* CLÉANTE) But you do not know that his consent is not
enough and that Heaven has given me back a brother (*points to* VALÈRE)
and a father (*points to* ANSELME) whose consent you need now.

ANSELME. I have not come back into your lives in order to oppose your
desires. Lord Harpagon, you must realize that a young girl will choose
the son rather than the father. Come now, don't force us to tell you
what you have no need to hear. Give your consent with mine to this
double marriage.

HARPAGON. I will make up my mind when I see my money box.

CLÉANTE. You will find it intact.

HARPAGON. I have no money to give to the marriage of my children.

ANSELM. Well, I have enough for them. Don't be concerned about this.

HARPAGON. Are you taking on the expense of these two marriages?

ANSELME. Yes, I give my word. Are you satisfied?

HARPAGON. Yes, provided you have new clothes made for me for the
wedding.

ANSELME. I agree. Now we must give over to the happiness of this
day. . . . Let us go now and tell your mother the joyous news.

HARPAGON. And let me go and see my beloved money box.

EXERCISES

Translate the following sentences into Latin, using the vocabulary supplied with each group of questions. You may also consult the Latin text of the play, the vocabulary at the end of the book, and a Latin dictionary, as needed.

Lines 1-39

1. I am the household Lar who has protected the grandfather and the father of the man now living in this house.
2. When the grandfather buried a treasure of gold in the hearth, he asked me to guard it.
3. That man was so greedy that he did not reveal the gold to his son, nor did the son reveal it to Euclio.
4. Although they did not honor me [present me with honors], the daughter of the family daily prays to me and gives me gifts.
5. Euclio has found the gold with my aid in order that the young man may marry Phaedria.
6. Phaedria was wronged by a man of very high rank whom she does not know.
7. Today the uncle of that young man will ask for Phaedria as his wife.

aurum auxilium avidus avunculus comprimere
dēfōdere honor impertīre indicāre neque
quamquam reperīre rogāre servāre supplicāre
thēsaurus

40-119

1. Euclio drives his slave Staphyla out of the house with harsh words.
2. Fearing that Staphyla might find his treasure, Euclio wanted very much to know that it was safe.
3. Since Staphyla knows about Phaedria's disgrace, she is afraid for the girl and for herself.
4. Having inspected his treasure, Euclio prepares to depart for the forum and orders the old woman to let no one into the house.
5. Euclio feels that everyone knows of his treasure hidden at home and therefore greets him in too friendly a way.

abscondere ācer aedēs anus benignē extrūdere
īnspicere magnopere metuere prō probrum reperīre
salvus thēsaurus

1. Eunomia thinks that her brother Megadorus ought to get married.
2. Megadorus refuses the woman with a very large dowry offered by Eunomia but says that he wishes to marry the daughter of the poor man Euclio even without a dowry.
3. As Euclio returns from the forum, anxious about his treasure, Megadorus asks for his daughter as his wife.
4. Euclio believes that Megadorus has found out about the gold because it is not by accident that a rich man seeks the favor of a poor man.
5. Finally the old man betroths his daughter on this condition, that no dowry be given.

arbitrārī aurum crēdere dēbēre dēspondēre dīves
dōs grātia lēx maximus negāre offerre pauper
poscere reperīre sine sollicitus temerārius thēsaurus

280-474

1. Cooks hired by Megadorus in the forum are led in by Strobilus along with flute girls, sheep, and provisions.
2. Having told various stories about the stingy Euclio, Strobilus divides his companions and provisions between the households of Megadorus and Euclio.
3. Congrio along with his assistants is driven out of the house by Euclio who has returned from the forum with only a little incense and floral garlands bought at little expense.
4. Having carried his pot of gold out of the house, Euclio allows Congrio to go inside to cook.
5. Euclio slaughtered Staphyla's cock because he thought that it tried to help the thieves.

adiuvāre agnus aula aurum comes cōnārī
condūcere coquere coquus corōna discipulus
dīvidere efferre emere extrūdere fābula familia
flōreus fūr gallus īnferre inīre minimus modo
obsōnium obtruncāre parcus redīre sinere sūmptus
tībīcina tūsculum ūnā varius

475-587

1. The friends of Megadorus think his plan about an undowered wife is a good one.
2. Megadorus proposes this plan in order that the state may become much more harmonious when rich men marry undowered daughters of poor men.
3. Euclio, listening to Megadorus, approves of what he says about the habits of dowered wives.
4. Euclio does not seem sufficiently well groomed for his daughter's wedding.
5. Suspecting that Megadorus knows about the gold, Euclio decides to entrust his treasure to Faith, whose shrine is next door.

aurum auscultāre cīvitās concors concrēdere
cōnsilium cōnstituere dīves dōtātus fānum Fidēs
fierī indōtātus intellegere mōs mulier nitidum
nūptiae pauper probāre prōpōnere proximus
suspicārī thēsaurus verbum

588-681

1. Lyconides' slave has been sent to spy out what is going on.
2. This slave tries to steal the treasure hidden by Euclio in the shrine of Faith.
3. Warned by a croaking raven, Euclio asks the slave whether he has stolen something from the shrine of Faith.
4. After Euclio decided to bury his gold in the grove of Silvanus, the slave ran ahead to see where the old man would bury his treasure.

abstrūdere aurum cōnārī cōnstituere corvus
dēfōdere fānum Fidēs fierī lūcus monēre num
postquam praecurrere speculārī surripere thēsaurus

682-end

1. Because the truth has now been told, Eunomia will ask her brother to announce the breaking of his engagement.
2. After having stolen the gold, Lyconides' slave goes home very joyfully to hide it.
3. Euclio and Lyconides converse in vain, the one about the lost gold, the other about the violation of Phaedria.
4. When Euclio discovers that his daughter has given birth and that Lyconides wishes to marry her, the grandfather finally consents to the marriage.
5. While Lyconides asks his slave about the theft, we are left in doubt since the end of the play has been lost.

abstrūdere alter aula aurum avus colloquī
comprimere cōnsentīre + ad + *acc.* dubium fābula
fīnis frūstrā fūrtum gaudium interrogāre maximus
nārrāre nūptiae parere perdere petere relinquere
remittere reperīre repudium surripere vērum

VOCABULARY

A

ā, ab (+ *abl.*), from, away from, by

abeō, -īre (*irreg.*), **-īvī** or **-iī, itum**, to depart

absēns, absentis, absent

*__absolvō, -vere__ (3), **-vī, -ūtum**, to release, pay off

*__abstrūdō, -dere__ (3), **-sī, -sum**, to conceal from view, hide

ac, and

accēdō, -dere (3), **-ssī, -ssum**, to go toward, approach

accipiō, -ipere (3), **-ēpī, -eptum**, to receive, accept

accūsō (1), to accuse

ad (+ *acc.*), to, toward, in, at

adeō (*adv.*), so, indeed, to such a degree, likewise

adeō, -īre (*irreg.*), **-īvī** or **-iī, -itum**, to come, approach

adsum, -esse (*irreg.*), **-fuī, -futūrus**, to be present, be near

adulēscēns, -ntis (*m*), young man

*__adveniō, -venīre__ (4), **-vēnī, -ventum**, to arrive, come

*__aedēs, -is__ (*f*), house (often in plural for a single house)

   *__aedīs = aedēs__

aequē, equally

*__aequus, -a, -um__, equal, fair, just, right

aes, aeris (*n*), copper, bronze, money

aetās, -ātis (*f*), age, time of life, life

*__afferō, -rre__ (*irreg.*), **attulī, allātum**, to bring

*__affīnis, -is__ (*m*), neighbor

*__age__, come now! come on!

ager, agrī (*m*), field

*__agitō__ (1), to move, stir, agitate

*__agnus, -ī__ (*m*), lamb

agō, agere (3), **ēgī, āctum**, to do, act, drive, treat

*__āiō, āis, ait, āiunt__, to say yes, say so, say

aliēnus, -a, -um, foreign, not belonging to the household

*__aliquī, aliqua__ (or **aliquae**), **aliquod**, some, any

aliquis, aliquid, someone, something, anyone, anything

alius, -a, -ud, other, another

   alius . . . alius, one . . . another

alter, -a, -um, the one, the other (of two), other

ambō, ambae, ambō, both

amīcus, -ī (*m*), friend

āmittō, -ittere (3), **-īsī, -issum**, to lose, send away, dismiss

amō (1), to love

*__amor, -ōris__ (*m*), love

amplius (*adv.*), more, more than

an, or

   an . . . an, either . . . or

*__angulus, -ī__ (*m*), angle, corner

*__anima, -ae__ (*f*), breath

animus, -ī (*m*), mind, courage, pride

annus, -ī (*m*), year

ante (+ *acc.*), in front of

*__anus, -ūs__ (*f*), old woman

aperiō (4), to open

appellō (1), to name, call, address, appeal to someone for something

apud (+ *acc.*), at, at the house of, with

aqua, -ae (*f*), water

*__arānea, -ae__ (*f*), cobweb

arbitror, -ārī (1), **-ātus sum**, to think, consider, observe

arbor, -oris (*f*), tree

*__argentārius, -ī__ (*m*), banker

*__argentum, -ī__ (*n*), silver, money

*__asinus, -ī__ (*m*), ass, donkey

*__aspiciō, -icere__ (3), **-exī, -ectum**, to catch sight of, observe

*__astō, astāre__ (1), **astitī**, to stand by, stand still at, but

atque, and, but

*__attat__: shortened form of **attatae**: interjection expressing sudden surprise

auctor, -ōris (*m*), promoter, sponsor, authority

audāx, -ācis, bold, daring

audeō, -dēre (2), **-sus sum**, to have a mind (to do something), be prepared, intend, dare

audiō (4), to hear

*__auferō, -rre__ (*irreg.*), **abstulī, ablātum**, to carry away, take away, steal

*aula, -ae (f), pot or jar for cooking
*aurum, -ī (n), gold
*auscultō (1), to listen to (+ accusative),
heed, obey (+ dative)
aut, or
   aut ... aut, either ... or
autem, moreover, however
auxilium, -ī (n), aid, help
*avidus, -a, -um, greedy, avaricious
*avunculus, -ī (m), mother's brother, mater-
nal uncle
*avus, -ī (m), grandfather

B

*bacchānāl, -lis (n), shrine or site where the
rites of Bacchus were celebrated
bene, well
*benignē, in a friendly spirit, kindly, pro-
fusely
*bibō, -ere (3), -ī, to drink
*blandē, cordially, in a fawning manner
bonus, -a, -um, good
*bōs, bovis (m), ox, bull

C

caedō, -dere (3), cecīdī, -sum, to cut down,
kill
capiō, -ere (3), cēpī, -tum, to take, seize,
hold
caput, -itis (n), head
*cārus, -a, -um, dear, expensive
causā (+ gen.), for the sake of
causa, -ae (f), cause, reason
caveō, -ēre (2), cāvī, cautum, to take precau-
tions, beware, take care
*cedo (imperative), give! hand over! bring!
cēdō, -dere (3), -ssī, -ssum, to come, go, go
away, give way, yield
celer, -ris, -re, swift
*cēlō (1), to hide, exclude someone from
knowledge of something
*cēna, -ae (f), dinner
cēnseō, -ēre (2), -uī, -um, to estimate, think,
decide
*Cerēs, -eris (f), the goddess of agriculture
certē, certainly
*certō, certainly, for a fact
certus, -a, -um, fixed, certain, sure
   certiōrem facere, to inform
   certum est, my mind is made up, I am
   sure
*cessō (1), to hold back from, hesitate
(+ infinitive)
cēterī, -ae, -a, the rest (of), the other
cīvis, -is (m), citizen
cīvitās, -ātis (f), state
clam (+ acc.), without the knowledge of
clāmō (1), to shout
*clāmor, -ōris (m), shout, shouting
*coctum: supine of coquō, expressing pur-
pose

coepī, -isse, -tum, began
cōgitō (1), to think, plan, think over, consider
cognōscō, -ōscere (3), -ōvī, -itum, to learn,
(perfect) to know
colligō, -igere (3), -ēgī, -ēctum, to collect
*colō, -ere (3), -uī, cultum, to live in, culti-
vate, tend
*comminīscor, -inīscī (3), -entus sum, to
think up
committō, -ittere (3), -īsī, -issum, to commit, entrust
commūnis, -is, -e, common
*comprimō, -imere (3), -essī, -essum, to press
tightly, make love with, rape
concēdō, -dere (3), -ssī, -ssum, to yield,
withdraw
*concrēdō, -ere (3), -idī, -itum, to entrust
something to someone (dative) for safekeeping
*condiciō, -ōnis (f), contract, match
*condō, -ere (3), -idī, -itum, to put away,
keep safe, bury, hide
*condūcō, -cere (3), -xī, -ctum, to bring to-
gether, hire, buy
cōnfīdō, -ere (3), -sus sum, to trust
*congredior, -dī (3), -ssus sum, to approach
*conqueror, -rī (3), -stus sum, to lament,
complain of
cōnsilium, -ī (n), plan, counsel
cōnsistō, -sistere (3), -stitī, to stand, stop,
halt
*cōnspicor, -ārī (1), -ātus sum, to catch sight
of, see
cōnsulō, -ere (3), -uī, -tum, to plan, consult
the interests of (+ dative)
*continuō (adv.), immediately
contrā, in return
controversia, -ae (f), dispute
*conveniō, -enīre (4), -ēnī, -entum, to come
together, visit, agree
cōpia, -ae (f), supply, abundance, resources,
possibility, chance
*coquō, -quere (3), -xī, -ctum, to cook
*coquus, -ī (m), cook
*cor, cordis (n), heart, mind
cornū, -ūs (n), horn (of animal)
*corōna, -ae (f), wreath
*corvus, -ī (m), raven
cotīdiē, daily
crās, tomorrow
crēber, -bra, -brum, thick
crēdō, -ere (3), -idī, -itum (+ dat.), to believe, entrust
*crepō, -āre (1), -uī, to make any kind of
loud noise
*crocōta, -ae (f), saffron-colored robe worn by
women
*crūdus, -a, -um, uncooked, raw
*crux, -ucis (f), cross (on which criminals
were exposed to die), plague, torment
*culpa, -ae (f), blame
*culter, -trī (m), knife
cum (+ abl.), with

cum, when, since, although
cupiō, **-ere** (3), **-īvī**, **-ītum**, to desire
cūr, why
cūra, **-ae** (f), care
cūrō (1), to care, care for, take care (of), see to it, cause
currō, **-rere** (3), **cucurrī**, **-sum**, to run
custōs, **-ōdis** (m), guard

D

*__damnum__, **-ī** (n), financial loss
dē (+ *abl.*), from, down from, concerning, about
dea, **-ae** (f), goddess
dēbeō (2), to owe, ought
dēcernō, **-ernere** (3), **-rēvī**, **-rētum**, to decide, decree
*__decet__, **-ēre** (2), **-uit** (*impersonal*), it is becoming, right, fitting
decimus, **-a**, **-um**, tenth
dēdo, **-ere** (3), **-idī**, **-itum**, to surrender, give up, hand over
*__dēfodiō__, **-odere** (3), **-ōdī**, **-ossum**, to bury (by digging down)
deinde, then, next
*__dēmō__, **-ere** (3), **-psī**, **-ptum**, to remove, take away, cut off
dēmōnstrō (1), to show, point out
*__deorsum__, down, down below
*__dērīdeō__, **-dēre** (2), **-sī**, **-sum**, to laugh at, make fun of
*__dēspondeō__, **-dēre** (2), **-dī**, **-sum**, to promise (a woman) in marriage, betroth
deus, **-ī** (m), god
dexter, **-era**, **-erum**, right (hand)
dextera, **-ae** (f), right hand
*__dī__ = **deī**
*__dīcitō__: future imperative
dīcō, **-cere** (3), **-xī**, **-ctum**, to say, tell
diēs, **-ēī** (m/f), day
dignus, **-a**, **-um**, worthy, worthy of (+ ablative)
*__dīmidium__, **-ī** (n), half
*__dispertiō__ (4), to divide up
*__dīves__, **-itis**, wealthy, rich
dīvidō, **-idere** (3), **-īsī**, **-īsum**, to divide
*__dīvitiae__, **-ārum** (f pl), riches, wealth
*__dīvus__, **-ī** (m), god
dō, **dare** (1), **dedī**, **datum**, to give
doceō, **-ēre** (2), **-uī**, **-tum**, to teach, show, tell
doleō (2), to grieve (at), be in pain, hurt
domus, **-ūs** (f), house, home
  domī, at home
  domō, from home
  domum, to home, home
*__dormiō__ (4), to sleep
*__dōs__, **dōtis** (f), dowry
*__dōtātus__, **-a**, **-um**, provided with a dowry
dubitō (1), to doubt, hesitate
dūcō, **-cere** (3), **-xī**, **-ctum**, to lead
*__dūdum__, just now
dum, while, until, provided

E

ē, **ex** (+ *abl.*), out of, from
*__ēbrius__, **-a**, **-um**, drunk
*__ēcastor__, by Castor
*__eccum__, here he is!
*__ecquid__ (*introducing a question*), surely
*__edepol__, by Pollux!
*__edō__, **esse** (*irreg.*), **ēdī**, **ēsum**, to eat
*__effero__, **-rre** (*irreg.*), **extulī**, **ēlātum**, to carry out, carry out for burial
*__effodiō__, **-odere** (3), **-ōdī**, **-ossum**, to dig up or out
ego, I
*__ei__, alas!
*__ēiulō__ (1), to shriek, wail
*__ēloquor__, **-quī** (3), **-cūtus sum**, to speak out, tell
*__em__, here you are! look at that!
*__ēmittō__, **-ittere** (3), **-īsī**, **-issum**, to send out, release, free
  manū ēmittere, to discharge a slave from one's power
emō, **emere** (3), **ēmī**, **ēmptum**, to buy
*__ēneco__ (1), to kill
enim, for, indeed
*__eō__, for this reason
eō, **īre** (*irreg.*), **iī** or **īvī**, **itum**, to go
*__equidem__, indeed, in truth
equus, **-ī** (m), horse
*__ergō__, therefore, then
*__erīlis__, **-is**, **-e**, of or belonging to a master
*__erus__, **-ī** (m), master
*__es__: imperative of **esse**
et, and
  et . . . et, both . . . and
etiam, also, even
etsī, even if, although
*__ēveniō__, **-enīre** (4), **-ēnī**, **-entum** (+ *dat.*), to happen to
ex, **ē** (+ *abl.*), out of, from
*__excūsō__ (1), to excuse
*__exeō__, **-īre** (*irreg.*), **-īvī** or **-iī**, **-itum**, to come or go out
exīstimō (1), to think
*__exquīrō__, **-rere** (3), **-sīvī**, **-sītum**, to ask about, inquire into
exstinguō, **-guere** (3), **-xī**, **-ctum**, to extinguish, put out
*__extemplō__, at once, immediately
extrā (+ *acc.*), outside of, beyond
*__extrūdō__, **-dere** (3), **-sī**, **-sum**, to force to go out, eject, expel

F

facilis, **-is**, **-e**, easy
*__facinus__, **-oris** (n), deed, act
faciō, **-ere** (3), **fēcī**, **factum**, to make, do, bring about, act
*__factum__, **-ī** (n), action, deed
*__fallō__, **-lere** (3), **fefellī**, **-sum**, to trick, mislead, lie

famēs, -is (f), hunger
familia, -ae (f), household
familiāris, -is, -e, of the household, family
*fānum, -ī (n), shrine
*fateor, -ērī (2), fassus sum, to admit
fēmina, -ae (f), woman
ferō, -re (irreg.), tulī, lātum, to bring, carry, bear, endure
ferrum, -ī (n), iron
fidēs, -eī (f), faith, trust
fīlia, -ae (f), daughter
fīlius, -ī (m), son
fīō, fierī (irreg.), factus sum, to be made, be done, become, happen
*focus, -ī (m), the hearth or fireplace in the atrium, the center of worship of the Lar familiāris
*forās, out-of-doors (always implying motion)
*foris, -is (f), door, (pl.) double door or its two leaves
*forīs, outside
forte, by chance
fortūna, -ae (f), fortune
*fortūnātus, -a, -um, successful, prosperous, lucky, wealthy
forum, -ī (n), public square in the center of a town, marketplace
frāter, -tris (m), brother
frōns, -ntis (f), front, forehead
*frūgī (indeclinable adj.), having merit or worth, honest, deserving
frūstrā, in vain
fugiō, -ere (3), fūgī, fugitum, to flee
*fullō, -ōnis (m), fuller, launderer
*fūr, -ris (m), thief
*fūstis, -is (m), stick, club

G

*gallinācius, -a, -um, domestic
*gallus, -ī (m), farmyard cock
gēns, -tis (f), tribe, nation
genus, -eris (n), kind, class, race, family
gerō, -rere (3), -ssī, -stum, to carry, do
  rem gerere, to carry on, do
*gradus, -ūs (m), step, pace
*grandis, -is, -e, grown up, old
*grātiā (+ gen.), out of consideration for, for the purpose of, for the sake of, on account of
grātia, -ae (f), favor, influence, gratitude, thanks
  grātiās habēre or agere, to be grateful, give thanks
*gula, -ae (f), throat, gullet, mouth

H

habeō (2), to have, hold, consider
habitō (1), to live, dwell
*haud, not

*heia (interjection expressing urgency), come on!
*hem (interjection indicating surprise, concern, or unhappiness), what's that? ah! alas!
*hercle, by Hercules!
*heus (interjection used to attract a person's attention), hey there!
*hīc (adv.), here
hic, haec, hoc, this
hinc, from here
*hodiē, today
homō, -inis (m), man, human being
honor, -ōris (m), honor, office
hūc, to this place, here

I

iaceō, -ēre (2), -uī, -itum, to lie, recline
iam, already, now, soon
iānua, -ae (f), door
ibi, there, in that place
īdem, eadem, idem, the same
idōneus, -a, -um, suitable
igitur, therefore, then
ignis, -is (m), fire
*ignōscō, -ōscere (3), -ōvī, -ōtum (+ dat.), to forgive
ille, illa, illud, that
*illic, illaec, illuc, that
*illūc, to that place, there
*immō (introducing the correction of a previous statement or question), rather, on the contrary
immortālis, -is, -e, immortal
imperium, -ī (n), command, power
imperō (1), to command, order
impetrō (1), to obtain (one's request)
*impleō, -ēre (2), -ēvī, -ētum, to fill something with something (+ genitive)
*improbus, -a, -um, shameless, presumptuous, insolent
in (+ abl.), in, on
in (+ acc.), into, among
*in rem esse, to be of advantage or in one's interest
*incēdō, -dere (3), -ssī, to step, walk, come
incipiō, -ipere (3), -ēpī, -eptum, to begin
inde, from there, then
*indicium, -ī (n), disclosure (of a fact), information
  indicium facere, to give away a secret
*indicō (1), to reveal, declare
*indōtātus, -a, -um, not provided with a dowry
īnferior, -ius, lower
*inhiō (1), to open one's mouth (for food), gape after
inimīcus, -ī (m), personal enemy
iniūria, -ae (f), wrong, injury
inquam, I say
īnsidiae, -ārum (f pl), ambush, plot
*īnspiciō, -icere (3), -exī, -ectum, to examine, inspect

intellegō, -gere (3), -xī, -ctum, to understand, know

inter (+ acc.), among, within, inside

intereō, -īre (irreg.), -īvī or -ii, -itum, to perish

interim, meanwhile

*intervīsō, -ere (3), -ī, -um, to go and see

*intrō, inside (with verbs implying motion)

*intus (adv.), inside

inveniō, -enīre (4), -ēnī, -entum, to come upon, find

invītus, -a, -um, unwilling

ipse, ipsa, ipsum, himself, herself, itself, themselves

    *ipse = dominus, the master himself, the master of the house

īrātus, -a, -um, angry

*irrīdeō, -dēre (2), -sī, -sum, to laugh at, mock

is, ea, id, this, that, he, she, it

iste, ista, istud, that (of yours)

*istīc (adv.), there, over there

*istic, istaec, istuc, that (of yours)

ita, so, thus

itaque, and so

item, likewise

iubeō, -bēre (2), -ssī, -ssum, to order

*Iūnō, -ōnis (f), Juno, the wife of Jupiter and queen of the gods

Iuppiter, Iovis (m), Jupiter, king of the gods

iūs, iūris (n), right, law

iūstus, -a, -um, just, right

L

labor, -ōris (m), toil, hardship, task

labōrō (1), to toil, struggle, suffer

*laevus, -a, -um, left, on the left hand

lapis, -idis (m), stone

*Lar, -ris (m), the tutelary god of hearth and home

latus, -eris (n), side, flank

laudō (1), to praise

*lavō (1), to wash, bathe

legiō, -ōnis (f), legion

lēx, lēgis (f), law, condition

*libēns, -ntis (adv.), willingly, gladly

līber, -era, -erum, free

līberī, -ōrum (m pl), children

*libet, -ēre (2), -uit or -itum est (impersonal), it is pleasing, agreeable

licet, -ēre (2), -uit or -itum est (impersonal), it is permitted, one may

*lignum, -ī (n), firewood

littera, -ae (f), letter of the alphabet

*locō (1), to put, place, give, give a girl in marriage to someone

locus, -ī (m), (pl) loca, -ōrum (n), place

longus, -a, um, long

loquor, -ī (3), locūtus sum, to speak, talk, talk about

*lūcus, -ī (m), sacred grove

lūx, lūcis (f), light

M

*macellum, -ī (n), market

magis (adv.), more

*magister, -trī (m), master, manager, official

magnus, -a, -um, large

maior, maius, larger, bigger, greater

*malam rem: "punishment"

*male (adv.), badly, severely, awfully

mālō, -lle (irreg.), -luī, to prefer

*malum, -ī (n), trouble, evil

malus, -a, -um, bad

maneō, -ēre (2), -sī, -sum, to remain, wait, wait for

manus, -ūs (f), hand

    *manū ēmittere, to discharge a slave from one's power

māter, -tris (f), mother

*mātrōna, -ae (f), married woman, matron

maximus, -a, -um, largest, greatest

*mecastor, by Castor!

*mēcum = cum mē

medius, -a, -um, middle (of)

melior, melius, better

*meminī, -inisse (perfect with present force), to remember

*memorō (1), to mention, speak of, tell

mēns, -tis (f), mind

mēnsis, -is (m), month

*mentiō, -ōnis (f), mention

*mercēs, -ēdis (f), wages, pay

mereō (2), to deserve, be worthy of

*meritō (adv.), deservedly

*metuō, -ere (3), -ī, metūtum, to fear

metus, -ūs (m), fear

meus, -a, -um, my, mine

*mī = mihi

mīles, -itis (m), soldier

*milvus, -ī (m), bird of prey, kite

minor, minus, smaller

    *minus, less

mīror (1), to wonder

miser, -era, -erum, wretched

mittō, -ere (3), mīsī, missum, to send, allow

modo, only, just, just now, lately

modus, -ī (m), amount, manner, way, measure, limit

*molestus, -a, -um, troublesome, annoying

moneō (2), to warn, advise

mōns, -tis (m), mountain

mora, -ae (f), delay

*mōrātus, -a, -um, endowed with character or manners (mōrēs) of a specific kind

moror, -ārī (1), -ātus sum, to delay

mors, -tis (f), death

*mortālis, -is (m), human being

mōs, mōris (m), custom, habit, (pl.) character

moveō, -ēre (2), mōvī, mōtum, to move

mulier, -eris (f), woman

multus, -a, um, much, (pl.) many

    multō, much

*mūlus, -ī (m), mule

mūrus, -ī (m), wall

mūtō (1), to change, exchange

N

nam, for

namque, for indeed, for

nāscor, -ī (3), **nātus sum**, to be born

*__nāta, -ae__ (f), daughter

*__nātus, -ī__ (m), son

-ne (*indicates a question*)

nē, that . . . not, lest, that, don't

nec, and not

negō (1), to say . . . not, deny

negōtium, -ī (n), business, trouble, problem

nēmō, nūllīus, nēminī, nēminem, no one

*__nempe__, without doubt, of course, to be sure

neque, and . . . not, nor

   neque . . . neque, neither . . . nor

*__nequeō, -īre__ (irreg.), **-īvī** or **-iī**, to be unable, be unable to (+ infinitive)

*__nesciō__ (4), not to know

nēve, and . . . not, nor

nihil (n), nothing

*__nīl = nihil__

*__nimis__, too much, too, very

nisi, unless, if . . . not

noctū, by night

nōlō, -lle (irreg.), **-luī**, to be unwilling, not wish

nōmen, -inis (n), name

nōn, not

*__nōn potest__, it is not possible

nōnus, -a, -um, ninth

nōs, we, us

nōscō, -scere (3), **nōvī, nōtum**, to become acquainted with, (perfect) know

noster, -tra, -trum, our, ours

nox, -ctis (f), night

*__nūbō, -bere__ (3), **-psī, -ptum**, (of a woman) to get married to

   nūptum dare, to give (someone) in marriage

*__nūgae, -ārum__ (f pl), idle talk, nonsense

   nūgās agere, to waste one's efforts, joke, jest, fool around

nūllus, -a, -um, no, not one

Num . . . ? (*introduces a question that expects the answer "no"*), Surely . . . not . . . ?

num, whether

numerus, -ī (m), number

*__nummus, -ī__ (m), coin, the silver didrachm used in the Greek cities of southern Italy

numquam, never

nunc, now

*__nunciam__, this very instant, here and now

*__nūptiae, -ārum__ (f pl), marriage ceremony and festivities, wedding

*__nusquam__, nowhere

*__nūtrīx, -īcis__ (f), nurse

O

*__ob__ (+ acc.), on account of, in front of

*__obeō, -īre__ (irreg.), **-īvī** or **-iī, -itum**, to meet with, come up against

mortem or **diem obīre**, to meet one's death, die

*__obsecrō__ (1), to pray, implore, beg

*__observō__ (1), to observe, note

*__obsōnium, -ī__ (n), provisions (of all sorts) for a meal

*__obsōnō__ (1), to purchase or get provisions, do the shopping

*__obtestor, -ārī__ (1), **-ātus sum**, to call upon as witness

occāsiō, -ōnis (f), opportunity

occīdō, -dere (3), **-dī, -sum**, to kill, ruin

*__occidō, -idere__ (3), **-idī, -āsum**, to fall or collapse in the way, die, be done for, be ruined

*__occipiō, -ipere__ (3), **-ēpī, -eptum**, to take up, begin

*__occlūdō, -dere__ (3), **-sī, -sum**, to close, shut (a door)

*__occultō__ (1), to hide, keep hidden, conceal

occultus, -a, -um, hidden

oculus, -ī (m), eye

officium, -ī (n), duty, job

omnis, -is, -e, all, every

   *__omnīs = omnēs__

onus, -eris (n), burden

*__onustus, -a, -um__ (+ gen. or abl.), burdened, loaded (with)

opera, -ae (f), effort, services

*__operam dare__, to pay attention to (+ dative), provide one's services

opīniō, -ōnis (f), belief, opinion

*__opīnor, -ārī__ (1), **-ātus sum**, to think, believe

oportet, -ēre (2), **-uit** (impersonal), it behooves, one ought

*__opperior, -īrī__ (4), **-tus sum**, to wait for

*__oppidō__, utterly, totally

optimus, -a, -um, best

*__opulentus, -a, -um__, wealthy, opulent

opus, -eris (n), work

opus est (+ acc. or abl.), there is need of

ōrātiō, -ōnis (f), speech

ordō, -inis (m), rank, row, arrangement, order, social class

orior, -īrī (4), **-tus sum**, to rise, arise

ōrō (1), to pray, beg, ask

ostendō, -dere (3), **-dī, -tum**, to show

P

*__pactum, -ī__ (n), agreement, manner, way

paene, almost

*__paenissimē__, very nearly

*__palam__, openly, publicly

   palam esse, to be generally known, common knowledge

   palam facere, to make known, divulge

   palam fierī, to become generally known

pānis, -is (m), bread

parcō, -cere (3), **pepercī, parsum**, to spare

*__parcus, -a, -um__, thrifty, stingy

*__pariō, -ere__ (3), **peperī, -tum**, to give birth

parō (1), to prepare

pars, -tis (f), part

*partitūdō, -inis (f), the act of giving birth
parvus, -a, -um, small, little
pateō, -ēre (2), -uī, to extend, be open
pater, -tris (m), father
patior, -tī (3), -ssus sum to allow, permit, suffer, endure
paucī, -ae, -a, few
*pauper, -eris, poor
*pauperiēs, -ēī (f), poverty
*peccō (1), to make a mistake, be wrong, do wrong
*pectus, -oris (n), chest, heart
pecūnia, -ae (f), money
pēior, pēius, worse
per (+ acc.), through, because of
*percontor, -ārī (1), -ātus sum, to question
*perditus, -a, -um, ruined, lost, done for
*perdō, -ere (3), -idī, -itum, to ruin, destroy, lose, waste
    operam perdere, to waste one's effort in doing something
pereō, -īre (irreg.), -iī, -itum, to perish, be lost, be wasted
perīculum, -ī (n), danger
*perscrūtor, -ārī (1), -ātus sum, to examine a person or place to find something hidden
*persequor, -quī (3), -cūtus sum, to follow persistently, pursue
perspiciō, -icere (3), -exī, -ectum, to perceive, see
pēs, pedis (m), foot
pessimus, -a, -um, worst
petō, -ere (3), -īvī or -iī, -ītum, to seek, beg
*Philippus, -ī (m), Philip II, king of Macedonia and father of Alexander the Great; Philip V of Macedon, defeated by the Romans at Cynocephalae in 197 B.C.
*pinguis, -is, -e, fat
*piscis, -is (m), fish
placeō (2), to please
*plēnus, -a, -um (+ gen.), full (of)
*plōrō (1), to lament, grieve, be distressed (to do something) (+ infinitive)
*plūrimus, -a, -um, most, (pl.) very many
*plūs (adv.), more
*pol, by Pollux!
polliceor, -ērī (2), -itus sum, to promise
pōnō, pōnere (3), posuī, positum, to put, place
populus, -ī (m), people, nation
poscō, -ere (3), poposcī, to demand, ask
possum, posse (irreg.), potuī, to be able, can
post (+ acc.), after, behind
post (adv.), afterward
posteā (adv.), afterward
postquam, after
postulō (1), to demand
*potest: nōn potest, it is not possible
potestās, -ātis (f), power
*potis or pote, possible
    pote (esse), to be possible
*potius . . . quam, rather than
*pōtō (1), to drink

praebeō (2), to furnish, offer, show
praeda, -ae (f), booty
*praedicō (1), to proclaim, declare
praefectus, -ī (m), officer, overseer
praetereā, besides, furthermore
*praetor, -ōris (m), praetor (a magistrate at Rome concerned chiefly with judicial functions)
*pretium, -ī (n), price, value
*prīdem, formerly, once
prior, -us, former, before
    *prius (adv.), formerly, before
priusquam or prius quam, before
prō (+ abl.), before, for, in behalf of, instead of, in return for, in proportion to, according to
*probē, properly, well
probō (1), to approve, prove
*probrum, -ī (n), disgrace, scandal
*profectō, without question, assuredly, absolutely
proficīscor, -icīscī (3), -ectus sum, to set out, start, depart
prohibeō (2), to prevent
*prōloquor, -quī (3), -cūtus sum, to speak forth
prope (adv.), near
*properē, quickly, without delay
*properō (1), to hurry, do, get ready with haste
propinquus, -a, -um, near
propter (+ acc.), on account of
proximē, most closely
*proximum, -ī (n), the immediate neighborhood or vicinity
    dē, ex, or ē proximō, from close at hand, neighboring, next door
puer, -erī (m), boy
pugna, -ae (f), fight
pulcher, -chra, chrum, beautiful
*pūrigō (1), to clean, purge oneself of an offense, apologize
*purpura, -ae (f), purple-dyed clothing
*puteus, -ī (m), well, pit for storing grain or confining prisoners
putō (1), to think

Q

quā, by which, where
*quadrilībris, -is, -e, containing four pounds of weight
quaerō, -rere (3), -sīvī or siī, -sītum, to seek, ask for
*quaesō, -ere (3), to try to obtain, seek, (idiomatically) "I ask you," "please"
*quālis, -is, -e, of what kind, quality, or sort?
quam, how, as, than, (with superlative) as . . . as possible
quamquam, although, and yet
*quandō, when
quantus, -a, -um, how great, how much, as great as
    quantum (adv.), as much as

*quasi, as, as if, just like
-que, and
*queō, quīre (irreg.), quīvī or quiī, to be able
*quī (old form of abl.), in order that by this means
quī, quae, quod, who, which, that, what
*quia, because, that
*quid = aliquid (after sī, num, or nē)
quidem, indeed, certainly, at least
quiētus, -a, -um, quiet
*quīn, indeed, in fact, even, why, but that, so as not to, that, that . . . not, why don't
quis (quī), (quae), quid, who? what?
*quis = aliquis (after sī, num, or nē)
quisquam, quicquam, anyone, anything, (as adjective) any
*quisquis, quidquid, whoever, whatever
quō, to which place, to what place, where
quōmodo, how
quoniam, since, when, after
quoque, also
*quōquō, wherever

R

rapiō, -ere (3), -uī, -tum, to snatch, steal
ratiō, -ōnis (f), reckoning, plan, reason, account, manner
*recipiō, -ipere (3), -ēpī, -eptum, to take back
    sē recipere, to take oneself back, return
*rēctē, rightly, well
reddō, -ere (3), -idī, -itum, to return, give back, make
redeō, -īre (irreg.), -īvī or -iī, -itum, to return, go back
redigō, -igere (3), -ēgī, -āctum, to drive or send back, reduce, bring back, restore
*referō, -rre (irreg.), rettulī, relātum, to bring back
relinquō, -inquere (3), -īquī, -ictum, to leave, leave behind, abandon
*renūntiō (1), to report, announce
reperiō, -īre (4), repperī, -tum, to find out, find
*repudium, -ī (n), repudiation or rejection of a prospective wife or husband, breaking of an engagement
rēs, reī (f), thing, matter, affair
    in rem esse, to be of advantage or in one's interest
    mala rēs, punishment
*respiciō, -icere (3), -exī, -ectum, to look back, look at
rēx, rēgis (m), king
rīdeō, -dēre (2), -sī, -sum, to laugh
*rogitō (1), to ask frequently or insistently
rogō (1), to ask
rūrsus, again, in turn

S

saepe, often
sagitta, -ae (f), arrow

salūs, -ūtis (f), safety
*salūtō (1), to greet
*salvus, -a, -um, safe, secure, unharmed
*sānē, soundly, certainly, truly
satis, enough, sufficiently
*scelestus, -a, -um, cursed, wicked, villainous
sciō (4), to know
scrībō, -bere (3), -psī, -ptum, to write
sē, himself, itself
sed, but
sedeō, -ēre (2), sēdī, sessum, to sit
semper, always
senātus, -ūs (m), senate
senex, -is (m), old man
sententia, -ae (f) opinion
sentiō, -tīre (4), -sī, -sum, to feel, perceive, think, have sense
sequor, -quī (3), -cūtus sum, to follow
*serviō, (4) (+ dat.), to serve, be a slave
servitūs, -ūtis (f), slavery
servō (1), to guard, protect, preserve
servus, -ī (m), slave
sēsē = emphatic sē
sī, if
sibi, to or for himself, for themselves
sīc, thus, so
sīcut, as if, just as
*Silvānus, -ī (m), Roman god associated with forest and uncultivated land
similis, -is, -e (+ gen.), like, similar
*simul, at the same time, together
simulō (1), to pretend
sine (+ abl.), without
*sinō, sinere (3), sīvī or siī, situm, to allow, let alone
*sīs = sī vīs, "if you wish," "please"
*situs, -a, -um, laid up, stored, deposited
sōl, sōlis (m), sun
soleō, -ēre (2), solitus sum, to be accustomed to, make it a practice to
*sollicitō (1), to disturb, trouble, worry
sōlus, -a, -um, alone, lonely, only
soror, -ōris (f), sister
spatium, -ī (n), distance, space of time
spērō (1), to hope, hope for
spēs, -eī (f), hope
*stimulus, -ī (m), goad, spur, sting, whip
stō, stāre (1), stetī, statum, to stand
*strophium, -ī (n), band worn by women under the breasts
studeō, -ēre (2), -uī (+ dat.), to be eager for, busy oneself with
stultus, -a, -um, stupid, foolish
sub (+ acc. or abl.), under, from under
*subveniō, -enīre (4), -ēnī, -entum (+ dat.), to come to one's assistance, help
sum, esse (irreg.), fuī, futūrus, to be
summus, -a, -um, highest, greatest
sūmō, -mere (3), -mpsī, -mptum, to take
*sūmptus, -ūs (m), expense, cost, charge
superō (1), to surpass, conquer
*surripiō, -ipere (3), -ipuī, -eptum, to snatch away secretly, steal

suspicor, -ārī (1), -ātus sum, to suspect
*sūtor, -ōris (m), shoemaker, cobbler
suus, -a, -um, his, her, its, their (own)

T

*taceō (2), to be silent
*tactiō, -ōnis (f), a touching, touch (used in Plautus as a verbal noun followed by an accusative object)
tam, so, so very
    tam . . . quam, as . . . as
tamen, nevertheless
*tandem, finally, now
tangō, -ere (3), tetigī, tactum, to touch
tantus, -a, -um, so great, so much, so many
*tēcum = cum tē
temptō (1), to test, try
teneō, -ēre (2), -uī, -tum, to hold, keep
    *tenē, tenē, stop him! stop him!
terra, -ae (f), earth
tertius, -a, -um, third
testis, -is (m), witness
*thēsaurus, -ī (m), hoard, treasure, store
*tībīcina, -ae (f), flute player
timeō, -ēre (2), -uī, to fear
tōtus, -a, -um, all, whole, entire
trēs, tria, three
tū, you
tum, then
*turba, -ae (f), disorder, crowd
tuus, -a, -um, your, yours

U

-ubi, where, when
ūllus, -a, -um, any
ultrō, besides, in addition, voluntarily
umquam (adv.), ever
unde (adv.), from where, from which place
*unguis, -is (m), fingernail, toenail
ūnus, -a, -um, one
usque, as far as, all the way
ut, that, how, as, when, whether, = utinam with subjunctive of wish
uter, utra, utrum, which (of two)
uterque, utraque, utrumque, both, each
*utinam: particle introducing a wish, expressed by the present subjunctive

ūtor, -ī (3), ūsus sum (+ abl.), to use, enjoy, experience
uxor, -ōris (f), wife

V

*vāh (interjection expressing astonishment), ah! oh!
valeō, -ēre (2), -uī, to be strong, be healthy
    valē, goodbye
*vāpulō (1), to be beaten
*vās, vāsis, (pl) vāsa, -ōrum (n), dish, utensil
*vehiculum, -ī (n), carriage
vehō, -here (3), -xī, -ctum, to carry
vel, even
veniō, venīre (4), vēnī, ventum, to come
*verberō (1), to lash, whip, beat
*verbum, -ī (n), word
    verba dare alicui, to give someone empty words, deceive, cheat
*vērō, truly
vertō, -tere (3), -tī, -sum, to turn, turn out, make something turn out
vērus, -a, -um, true
    vērum, -ī, and vēra, -ōrum (n), the truth
*vērum, but truly
vester, -tra, -trum, your (pl.)
vestis, -is (f), clothing
vetus, -eris, old
via, -ae (f), road, way
*vīcīnus, -ī (m), neighbor
videō, vidēre (2), vīdī, vīsum, to see, (passive) seem
*vigilia, -ae (f), wakefulness, watching, military guard, nightly vigils at religious festivals
*vīlis, -is, -e, cheap
vīlla, -ae (f), farm(house)
vīnum, -ī (n), wine
vir, virī (m), man
*virgō, -inis, unwedded, (as a noun) unwedded woman
virtūs, -ūtis (f), courage
    virtūte (+ gen.), thanks to, in virtue of
vīta, -ae (f), life
vīvō, -vere (3), -xī, -ctum, to live
vīvus, -a, -um, alive, living
vocō (1), to call
volō, velle (irreg.), voluī, to wish, be willing
vōx, vōcis (f), voice